'In essence we all "reap w~~...~~ ~~.. ~~.. ~~...~~ and are a product
of the choices we make. This book will help us make the
right choices in living a life of freedom with God.'
*Martin Smith, Delirious?*

'Pithy, focused and down-to-earth, Matt Bird's book is an
admirable backpack for Christians who really want to set
out for spiritual adventure.'
*Richard Chartres, Bishop of London*

'Fresh and inspiring, this essential look at the issues facing
Christians today is a great follow-on from Matt's first
book, *Destiny*.'
*Mike Pilavachi, Director, Soul Survivor*

'A very readable and important book for every young
person – and parent! I wish I had read this before our
children became teenagers. It presents the case for
traditional morality in contemporary language.'
*R. T. Kendall, Minister, Westminster Chapel*

'So many Christians' lives are lived in the "land of the
bland". This book will help plot a journey to a new place
of authentic, energised Christian life.'
*Phil Wall, National Evangelist, Salvation Army*

'This book is not for those looking for a safe and com-
fortably religious sort of read. Punchy, uncompromising
and in places very funny, it challenges the way in which
we engage with living and argues powerfully for an
authentic discipleship that is rooted in the everydayness
of twenty-first-century culture. It's well worth reading!'
*Fran Beckett, Chief Executive, The Shaftesbury Society*

'Powerful, practical and pertinent; a challenging and
refreshing read.'
*Lyndon Bowring, Executive Chairman, CARE*

'Thoughtful and thought-provoking.'
*Sally Magnusson, Broadcaster*

'*Manifesto for Life* deals with running for Jesus in the world, rather than running from the world and never discovering the full adventure of being a disciple. Matt Bird gets to grips with some major topics and offers sound suggestions for practical discipleship.'
*David Coffey, General Secretary, Baptist Union of Great Britain*

'Matt Bird's new book, *Manifesto for Life*, tackles many of the issues which today's 20s and 30s are facing. It does so with wit, practical advice and personal illustration. At a time of new parliamentary manifestos it is good to see something which hits everyday people where they are at.'
*Rob Frost, National Evangelist, Rob Frost Team*

'Competing voices, images and messages can distract the most sincere, passionate follower of Christ. If you feel sometimes distracted or are in danger of losing your way this is the book to read. It is up-to-date, relevant and sometimes right in your face. Matt Bird provides the focus we all need.'
*Gerald Coates, Team Leader, Pioneer*

'Matt Bird has done it again! This book will help all Christians trying to follow Christ in a fast-moving, ever-changing world. Full of anecdotes and practical insights, his book will make a real difference to many lives.'
*Gary Streeter, MP for South West Devon*

'Again Matt's common-sense street wisdom and biblical truth produce an easily edible yet nourishing entrée to strengthen us in following Jesus in the twenty-first century. Ingest the inspiration immediately!'
*Roger Forster, Leader, Icthus Christian Fellowship*

# Manifesto for Life

## A transforming lifestyle for the twenty-first century

## Matt Bird
### with Craig Borlase

Hodder & Stoughton
LONDON SYDNEY AUCKLAND

First published in Great Britain in 2001

The right of Matt Bird and Craig Borlase to be identified as
the Authors of the Work has been asserted by them in accordance
with the Copyright, Designs and Patents Act 1988.

10 9 8 7 6 5 4 3 2 1

British Library Cataloguing in Publication Data
A record for this book is available from the British Library

ISBN 0 340 75673 X

Typeset by Avon Dataset Ltd, Bidford-on-Avon, Warks

Printed and bound in Great Britain by
The Guernsey Press Co. Ltd, Channel Isles

Hodder & Stoughton Ltd
A Division of Hodder Headline Ltd
338 Euston Road
London NW1 3BH

# Contents

# *Foreword*

Silviane lives in Haiti.

She was only sixteen years old when she was raped. The perpetrator of the abuse was the man for whom she worked as a domestic servant. She left the house, but two or three months later found out to her horror that she was pregnant as a result of the rape.

After the birth, and now with a child to look after, she found that the only way to survive was through prostitution. She would sell her body for 10 Haitian gourdes, a bit over one pound sterling. The inevitable result was more children, and from unknown fathers. The end of that chapter of the story was that she found it necessary to work the streets all day long in order to feed her little family.

After six years of having to live in this fashion, she found herself occupying a little shack in a slum. This notorious area was actually adjacent to the headquarters of the Lemuel Project, an indigenous evangelical organisation, set up to offer care and support for those living in such squalid conditions. Its director, a warm and approachable Haitian man named Manis, has a simple rule for the staff who are involved with the project. He insists that there is to be no verbal attempt at direct evangelism until people are first asking questions for themselves. His conviction is that Christian lives should provoke inquiry, not for what we avoid, but from the way in which we actually live. So evangelism in this community developed from the interest created by the compassionate care which typifies the lives of the Christians. The only exceptions Manis feels obligated to make to this rule are those suffering from AIDS or others among the chronically sick. Those who may just not have enough time left are told of Jesus immediately.

Gigi Munchmore, an American nurse who has lived in Haiti for thirty-seven years, met and then befriended Silviane. After several months she was eventually asked the bitter and honest question, 'What are you trying to get from me?' The answer came back that instead of trying to exploit Silviane, Gigi was trying to give her something, and led Silviane to commit her life to Jesus.

Today, Silviane's home is still the tiny and primitive hut in the shanty town in Port au Prince. She shares a single room with her five children – though, because she is given to hospitality and is reluctant to see off people who have absolutely nowhere to go, at times as many as eight people will live in that one room. This room is all the dwelling consists of. Loosely speaking, it is constructed with discarded pieces of used plywood or tin. Yet Silviane's pride and joy is a new section of tin sheeting that actually has no holes in it. Joining in her weekly small group fellowship meeting, she wants everyone to share her joy and thank God with her, because she now has a small corner of her room in which she can sit and not get wet when it rains! This is what can happen when Christians live Jesus and do not just hide behind a form of words – however doctrinally correct they may prove to be.

This is exactly the issue that Matt Bird addresses in this fine little book. For many, this 'post-modernity' is little more than a word, but for whole new generations of young people in our world today, it is the very society in which they have to live and breathe. There is little point in us engaging in philosophical discussion on the issue. We need to equip people to live in today's world.

For this reason I genuinely believe that every single youth group in an evangelical church in Britain today should have a copy of this book available for its members. For in his typical, unafraid fashion, Matt engages in a lively discussion of how we really do live today in God's world, God's way.

So many of our young people are besieged by a whole new generation of problems, attitudes and world views. To read in these pages of how to confront that world, respond to that world and love that world with the care and compassion of Jesus is eye-opening – and could be life-changing in its consequences.

I've often been asked to write a foreword to a book. You struggle to say nice things about the author and about its contents. But standing outside a Haitian shack and learning of how someone came to Jesus, not through words but through a life lived for Him, was reminiscent of how I myself had come to faith. In a post-modern world, people are increasingly impressed by images, pictures and reality lived out in front of them. This is not to deny the truth of the propositional phrases contained in Scripture. It is just that the Word of God deserves not only to be read but also to be lived!

We today have the obligation of being the hands and feet of Jesus. I guess that these pages will help us all to catch hold of that idea and live for Him, so that the Silvianes of tomorrow might also find Jesus as their saviour and friend.

Clive Calver

# *Thanks*

To my team: Matt Stuart for cheering for me as I cheer for you, and Mary Johnson for helping me squeeze in writing among everything else.

To my encouragers: Steve Clifford, Paul Williams and many others for loving me and believing in who I am and what I do.

To those who commented on parts of the manuscript of this book: Esther Jenkins, Richard Tiplady, Jon and Kirsty Jolly, Amanda Collins, Claire Mirriam, Shane Mullins and others.

To Craig Borlase, for your special talent with words, and to my editor David Moloney, for running with another of my ideas.

# *Introduction*

*Manifesto for Life* is a book about discipleship. Not discipleship within the safe confines of the Christian community, but discipleship in the unlimited space of the world that surrounds us.

*Manifesto for Life* explores the nit and the grit of nine key lifestyle issues that face us all today. How did I choose them? I cheated. I emailed a large number of mates and asked them to tell me what they felt were the key issues facing them as Christians today. A whole load of topics came back and, give or take a few, they can all be found in the following pages.

Let's just get a few things straight before we kick off. First, discipleship is not about rules. It's not a composite of 'dos' and 'don'ts', nor is it about 'do what you like'. It's not about legalism or liberalism, but a love affair with Jesus Christ. True discipleship is based on living a life that pleases our Father in heaven.

Second, it's all about grace, not about law. The way forward in the Christian faith is the same as the way in: in other words, by grace. Things don't change as we try and get closer to God – at no point do we deserve it. Our position with God is based solely on his outrageous and extravagant love that lets us ever closer.

Third, we need to remember that discipleship is about being God's partners, not his puppets. The will of God is not to control who we were designed to be, but to liberate us to discover all that he created us to be. Genuine Christianity never robs us of our personality: it helps us discover it.

It's about being in an adventure park, not balancing on a tightrope. The will of God is large, not small. It encompasses a multitude of choices, and at each point we are asked whether we are living for God or ourselves.

Finally, discipleship depends on our being willing and able to adapt to the culture that surrounds us, not fighting it off. God didn't send Jesus because he hated the world, but because he loves it. Discipleship is about learning to incarnate the gospel, discovering the way of living a life that follows Jesus' lead in our life, communities and work.

If those things resonate with you, you will have fun reading *Manifesto for Life*. If not, I hope it will stir you to think about things that you might otherwise have passed over. And if that doesn't work, I hope at least that you'll be able to get your money back.

# 1
## *Identity and Image*

**The scene**

Listen to the ad man and what do we hear? A simple, none-too-subtle message: we are defined by the products we use. If we drink a certain vodka, drive a certain car or visit a certain country we will become a certain person. And what does that person look like? Slim, healthy and infinitely attractive to whichever sex takes their fancy. Not a bad result for a few simple purchases, huh?

Visiting the cinema gives the opportunity of playing the Guess The Product game. The rules are surprisingly simple: sit through the ad and guess the product. Often I've been amazed at the tenuous link between the apparently random collection of lifestyle images and the finished product. Lately, however, it seems as though many have done away altogether with pretending that the product needs to fit in with the narrative. After all, why bother complicating things when a blatant message will do the trick? And so there we have it: shots of beautiful bodies (cue thought: 'I want that for myself') leading beautiful lives (cue thought: 'I want that for myself') followed by random product (cue thought: 'I can have the body and lifestyle if only I buy that particular brand of ceramic tile adhesive').

But it doesn't stop with advertising. Its close cousin, fashion, also tries to sell us an identity, this time suggesting that the labels we wear send out certain messages. Of course, they're right: everything we wear tells others about ourselves – from the cut of our hair to the style of our wardrobe. Trouble enters the room, however, when we believe that it's the labels themselves that provide our image, that self-worth can only come with a decent wardrobe.

Education gets in on the act by telling us that we are defined by the qualifications we have gained. Parental pressure is just one of the factors that can make study such a stressful time; add in worry about the future and peer competition and you've got a tasty little cocktail just waiting to mess with your head.

Consumerism delicately suggests that it is our shopping experiences that define us. Do we shop successfully? Do we have a decent spread of gold and platinum cards in our wallet? Do we have a home filled with desirables? Do we partake in regular spending sprees to rid our bank accounts of wads of money? We do? Well done.

Then there's that part within us that some people like to call our conscience. That tells us that we are defined by our mistakes. Bad relationships? Then we become a romantic failure. Lost a job? Unemployable. Spent too much time having fun while we should have been working? We'll never amount to anything. In the universe of conscience we can lose touch with forgiveness and the possibilities of new beginnings.

Of course, we can't forget career, which tells us that our identity is defined by success. This can be a tricky one for Christians as God's idea of success plays – I'm convinced – by a completely different set of rules to the cultural norm. Jesus was the master of turning the accepted ways on their head, and he made sure that we got the message loud and clear. Annual media events like the publication of *The Times* Power List, the World's Most Influential 100 or the World's Richest give a fascinating insight into the gauges we use to judge success. I wonder what Jesus has to say about them . . .

The social class system would have us believe that we are defined by the clues we drop: the accent, aspirations or background. Some are not so subtle, as a name-drop of a certain school, college, holiday destination or car will send a clear message about who we want people to think we are.

The cosmetics and beauty industry tells us that we are defined by our appearance, and we hope the mirror will confirm our membership of the Beautiful People Club.

Sexuality tells us that our identity is wrapped up in us being 'in relationship'. If we're in a relationship then bully for us, but should we happen to be single then I'm afraid we're not complete and there must be something wrong with us. So it's back at the bottom of the pile.

Then there's Christianity. What does it have to say about

our identity? The answer is simple: we are defined by our origins in God.

## Origins

'Then God said, "Let us make humankind in our image, in our likeness".'

Genesis 1:26

In truth, all of the above – from ads to beauticians, fashion to class – contribute to our identity. It is not possible for us to be immune from the effects of our experience of life and the stuff that surrounds us. However, this isn't a cue for us to get out the emotional secateurs and do some internal pruning, cutting and casting out anything that hasn't got God explicitly written through it like the words in a stick of rock. What we can do, though, is to remember Jesus' words: 'For where your treasure is, there your heart will be also' (Matthew 6:21). Whatever we've signed up for with the greatest enthusiasm, then that's where we can find our heart, that's where we believe our identity lies.

Christianity isn't just another alternative identity provider. Christianity tells us where we have come from and why we are here. God has created us and we have our root identity in him. Just look at your friends and acquaintances: they're all different, and if you think about it, in fact each one is incredibly special and unique. God has defined our DNA. He is the origin of our personality, style, temperament and talents. He is also the origin of the creation that surrounds us, which as we engage with it adds to our identity.

It is true that creation has been made in the image of

God, and that image has sadly been corrupted and spoilt. As the characters in *The Matrix* realise Neo's (Keanu Reeves) true identity, the claim is made that 'he is the one'. So it is with us: Jesus is the one who has come to restore the world to the image of God. *And* he knows kung fu.

Before I became a Christian I was quiet, timid and unsure. Meeting Jesus gave me confidence to be the person I was created to be. The experiences that had hurt and hindered me – while still being there – were no longer the defining forces of my life. Instead, I was a son of the Father, a child of God, an heir of the King, ready to discover more of the rich inheritance that was laid on for me.

If identity is our inherent personality and uniqueness, then image is that which we choose to present to other people. Within both of these it's vital that we understand more of how Jesus sees us so that we might have greater security and self-worth. It is possible to care about your image at the same time as knowing your identity. The most 'together' people are confident to allow their true identity to be shown in their image. Others have to undertake the journey of self-discovery allowing God to clean up on the way, so they can allow the beauty that is inside to come out. After all, as Jesus himself said:

> 'Love the Lord your God with all your heart and with all your soul and with all your mind.' This is the first and greatest commandment. And the second is like it: 'Love your neighbour as yourself.' All the Law and the Prophets hang on these two commandments.
>
> Matthew 22:37–40

At times it has profoundly puzzled me why Jesus told us to 'love your neighbour as you love yourself'. I was under the impression that Christianity was partly about being selfless. The truth is that if we don't love ourselves – if we don't have a healthy sense and appreciation of who we are in Jesus – then we will find it difficult to love and appreciate others. This dawned on me one day when I realised that there was a reason why I was always very hard on other people: it was because I was hard on myself. In order to be kind to others I had to learn to be kind to myself, and to be kind to myself I needed to experience the kindness and generosity of God in a new and dynamic way.

Yet all this has to be seen in context. 'Life' – as M. Scott Peck announced at the start of *The Road Less Travelled* – 'is difficult.' The pressures that face us, particularly those pressures of identity, exert a force that is almost impossible to resist. So many of us don't like who we are, and almost all of us would rather upgrade some part of our person for a better model, whether that be physical, mental or emotional. Unfortunately, what we need is not a six-pack and a size eight, but (and excuse me if I'm sounding a little blissed-out here) happiness. We need to learn to be happy with our bodies, happy with ourselves.

One of my favourite psalms says this:

Yahweh, investigate my life. Get all the facts first hand – I'm an open book to you. Even from a distance you know what I'm thinking. You know when I leave and when I get back. I am never out of your sight. You know everything I'm going to say before I start the first sentence. I look behind me and you're there, then up ahead and you're there too, your reassuring presence coming and going. This is too much! Too wonderful! I can't take it all in. Is there any place I can go to avoid your spirit, to be out of your sight? If I climb to the sky you're there. If I go underground you're there. If I flew on morning's winds to the far western horizon you'd find me in a minute. You are already there waiting. Then I said to myself 'Oh, he even sees me in the dark. At night I am immersed in the light.' It's a fact; darkness isn't dark to you. Night and day, dark and light; they're all the same to you. Oh yes, you shaped me first inside, then out. You formed me in my mother's womb.

Psalm 139, *The Message*

God knows us inside out. He knitted us together in our mother's womb. Even those of us who are a slip of family planning are not really an accident. God knew who we were going to be long before our parents jumped into bed together, or wherever they did it (what a horrible thought – let's not go there . . .). It is true that God designed us, that he created us, that he knows us better than we know ourselves. God knows every email we send and receive, the transactions of our bank accounts, the tugs and pulls of our hearts, every stray and straight thought, and what goes on in our bedrooms. God knows us intimately and he defines our identity.

This is important stuff. With the firm base of a sound knowledge of who we are in God, friendships, relationships and career will beat to the rhythm of a new song. Instead of taking clues about our identity from a myriad of sources, compiling them like a shopping list scribbled on the back of an envelope, we will be able to stand firm, secure in who we are.

Our identity is tied up in function, or to put it another way, our journey of self-discovery defines our destiny. However, it is critical that who we are is more important than what we do, that our identity precedes our function. This is the ultimate security in God: however we are pushed and pulled through the adventure of life, we are rock solid in knowing that we are in God and God is in us. Personally speaking, my closest friends are those who know and love Matt the person; they are people who know my mistakes and my eccentricities and still love me. They cheer and encourage me in chasing my destiny, but it doesn't matter how close I get to achieving my goals: their friendship is unconditional. We are most secure when our identity is in who God has made us to be rather than what God has asked us to do.

In my previous book, *Destiny*, I explored how each of us is born for a reason and how God has a unique calling and destiny for each of our lives. This destiny flows out of our God-given identity: who God has made us to be defines what God has made us to do. The creation mandate is about our identity and destiny . . .

Then God said, 'Let us make humankind in our image, in our likeness, and let them rule over the fish of the sea and the birds of the air, over the livestock, over all the earth, and over all the creatures that move along the ground.' So God created humankind in his image. In the image of God male and female he created them.

Genesis 1:26

Humankind is created with an identity in the image and likeness of God so that we can enjoy relationship with each other and a destiny to rule, serve and lead creation. Our manifesto for life is defined in the creation mandate – to know our life origins and purpose. We will only discover the fullness of who we are as we pursue our destiny. As I travel around the world I meet many people who are living in their destiny, and their identity sings and shouts out to everyone they meet. There are other people who may know who they are in God but are still only half a person because they haven't yet discovered their God-given destiny. When we discover our destiny we discover to a greater degree our identity. Identity is tied up in function: identity must precede function, but complete identity can only be known in our destiny. Don't worry if this all sounds a bit much as we'll come back to destiny and vocation in more detail in the next chapter.

So many members of our generation have a personality that is completely confused. We're unsure not only about who we are, but about why we're here and what life is about. Some thought the millennium might be a line in the sand, with the other side representing significance and fulfilment. Unfortunately, all the twenty-first century seems to have offered so far has been more of the same: more conflict, more injustice, more confusion. The PMT (pre-millennial tension) has been followed swiftly by PMV (post-millennial vacuum), and we're left clearing up the party poppers and wondering where it all went.

Holding up a mirror to this has been popular culture. The arts have responded to the sense of futility that seems to be kicking around the place, with a couple of notable winners. There was the character in *Fight Club* played by Edward Norton, articulating this position beautifully. The banality of his existence and near total absence of any sense of meaning or purpose from his life led him on meaningless binges. From the IKEA catalogue to the brutal fighting in deserted car parks, he searched for something to underline his existence as worthwhile.

Then there was Douglas Coupland's book *Miss Wyoming*. It charts the story of Susan Colgate – winner of a hundred teenage beauty pageants and child star of an all-American soap, *Meet the Blooms* – and John Johnson – action film star, director, occasional sado-masochist and junkie. Their lives are a frenzy of massive success and personal failure. Each of them is searching for meaning, deciding en route to drop out and pursue an answer to the eternal 'why?' Both attempt reinventing or reconstructing their identity but both ultimately fail, leaving them to come to terms with their past, family and careers in order to re-emerge into society. Eventually they find in each other someone who accepts them for who they are, not for who they try to be. Setting a novel with this theme in Hollywood was a masterstroke.

In Jesus we can be restored in our God-given identity and destiny. Jeremiah the prophet reassured the people of God at a time in their lives when they had been snatched from their own city and culture and exiled to a strange place. They were struggling to know their identity and destiny, much like many of us today: ' "For I alone know the plans I have for you," declares the Lord, "plans to prosper you and not to harm you, plans to give you hope and a future" ' (Jeremiah 29:11).

Know, hear and feel the reassurance of God for you in who he has made you to be and what he is asking you to do.

## Parenthood

As we've looked at already, the greatest factor in defining our identity is knowing God and who we are in him. Knowing this, Paul wrote to the church at Galatia: 'But when the time had fully come, God sent his Son, born of a woman, born under law, to redeem those under law, that we might receive the full rights of sons. Because you are sons, God sent the Spirit of his Son into our hearts, the Spirit who calls out, "*Abba,* Father" ' (Galatians 4:4–6).

Talking of Abba, I really enjoyed the show *Mamma Mia* (OK, it was a cheesy link). For weeks after seeing the West End hit I was blasting the music out of my car, singing blissfully along to those Abba classics. Of course, the windows and the roof were tightly closed as I drove through residential areas – not for fear of disturbing the residents, you understand, but for fear of appearing a total pillock. The musical followed the story of Sophie, who lived with her mother on a Greek island. She was about to be married and desperately wanted her father to be at the ceremony. She found her mother's diaries from the summer she was conceived, and looking through realised that her father could be one of three men. She invited them all to the wedding, to find out which one was her father so that he might give her away. Mere musical-fodder? Perhaps, but the need to know who we are and where we've come from is a river that runs deep and fast within each of us. Where we come from really counts.

While a 'stable' family background offers no guarantees when it comes to the security of the child, it has been often suggested that marriage is the best frame within which to bring up children. Of course, a marriage where arguments and violence are the norm won't do anyone much good, but the point is there to be made: those who have benefited from a strong and loving family where unconditional love and affirmation are part of the daily fabric are off to a good start. That doesn't mean that single parents can't bring up children perfectly well on their own, but they are the first to say it's a bigger challenge. The family unit is the ideal model for the nurture of children. I suppose the trouble is that we don't seem to be living in an ideal world.

However, if you're like me and come from a difficult family background we have the promise that God is a father to the fatherless, a parent to those who've lost out, as Psalm 68 makes clear. This was a great comfort to me when I explained to my dad that I was leaving my job in the Ministry of Defence in favour of spending a year at Bible college. His reaction hurt me: at first he thought I was joking. When he realised I wasn't, he told me that if I was going to jack in the career I wasn't to come back home or to expect any sort of support from him. College was a pretty raw time for me, but one morning a friend came by, telling me that God had woken her in the middle of the night. He gave her the words and music for a song from him to me, and she sat down and sang it there and then:

> O my child are you hurt,
> I can feel your pain.
> O my child I understand,
> I have been there too
> standing beside you.
> Simply because I love you.

My dad plainly didn't want to know, and it was amazing to discover the fatherhood of God in such a meaningful way. God my Father was more than willing and able to be my dad, looking out for me, providing for my needs, advising me and – most important – loving me to bits. There is so much the Father has for us: the promise that all things work out for the good of those who love him, and the knowledge and experience of his outrageously unconditional love.

God rejoices over us, taking huge delight in who we are. Don't believe me? Read Zephaniah 3:17 for yourself. Alternatively, you can get a picture of it from the old Steve Martin film *Parenthood*. Towards the end he's watching his son play baseball, and he's delighted to see junior catch the final ball, winning the game for his team. Steve Martin's character is over the moon and does the most amazing dance of celebration across the field: punching the air, bouncing on his knees, falling prostrate and finally scooping up his son. What a wonderful picture of true parental love – a fraction of the sort that God has for us. Just one point, though: God would have had the same reaction even if the boy had dropped the ball.

There are characteristics about God that are closer to our traditional cultural models of motherhood. God can comfort, nurture and cherish. Isaiah talks about some of these in chapter 49: 'Can a mother forget the baby at her breast and have no compassion on the child she has borne? Though she may forget, I will not forget you! See, I have engraved you on the palms of my hands' (Isaiah 49:15).

And again in chapter 66: 'As a mother comforts her child, so will I comfort you; and you will be comforted over Jerusalem' (Isaiah 66:13).

It's wonderful to think of God like that: dependable, comforting, capable. Perhaps your mum is similar to mine, fiercely proud. Even when I wasn't a Christian and had not discovered who I was in God, my mum was always proud of me. Even now that I feel as if I've discovered more of my identity and destiny in God, my mum's still just as proud. It's good to think of God like that, especially as his arms are even stronger than those of any of our earthly mothers.

Finally, it's important to remind ourselves of the truth that God promises to set the lonely in families. Whether we've got our own families or whether we haven't, whether we've had good experiences of them in the past or bad ones, God is in the business of making us aware of just how much a part of his family we are. On a practical level this has meant that, on many different occasions, I have been struck by the openness of plenty of families. It might have meant being invited for Sunday dinner, or getting a Christmas Day invite at the beginning of December instead of at the last minute like some sort of charity case. With some other people, it might have meant just being made aware of the fact that their doors are always open. God sets the lonely in families.

### Life action

1 Choose somewhere picturesque where you can take a stroll and relax. Pause and ponder before God who you are. What are the personality, temperament, personal style and talents God has given you? Pray and offer all of who you are to him who made you.

2 Take time with a friend and talk about what you like as well as what you struggle with about yourself.

3 Pray and ask God to reveal more of your destiny and identity.

# 2
# *Work and Career*

**The scene**
Pressures at work? Nothing new. Feeling the heart-rate move a few points up the scale once you're in the office? Join the club. Too much to do in too little time with too little support? There's a queue.

The fact is that many of us are facing an increasing amount of stress in the workplace. Whether it's the uncertainty of the short-term contract, the risk-related pressures of self-employment or the responsibilities of working towards someone else's agenda, our non-leisure time can occasionally feel like a regular well-spring of aggravation. And, of course, it's not just when we're in work that things are tough; a period of unemployment – no matter how long – will bring with it doubts and questions that begin the steady process of eroding our self-esteem. Face facts, honey, this work thing can be tough. Makes me just want to go and find a beach somewhere. Mmm. What a good idea.

Three years ago I moved to London. I was skint (obviously) and desperate for work. Fortunately I managed to get a job with someone I knew well. Everything was going fine – the job paying the bills while I concentrated on setting up Joshua Generation – until I was told that, effective immediately, my hours had been cut in half and that they would disappear altogether within a couple of months. The organisation had a cash flow problem, and being the last in, I was the first out. Again I was fortunate: within a couple more months I had generated more work for myself and was back on track, but for a while the worry weighed heavy on my mind.

Of course, this is neither unusual nor dramatic. Many of us have lost more for longer, endured worse with less hope or spent even longer searching for the light at the end of the proverbial tunnel. The job market has changed and, regardless of whether we like it or not, there's no such thing as a job for life any more. It's estimated that our generation of workers can expect to go through an average of three major career (not just job) changes throughout our working lives. Think back a couple of generations: how many of our parents or grandparents had that kind of work pattern?

Of course, this can be one of those glass half full/glass half empty situations: we've got either increased choice or decreased security. While the optimist in me likes to rejoice at the prospect of shifting career along with the changing tides of my taste, I'm convinced that the vastly increased potential to get truly shafted by the job market may outweigh the apparent delights of choice. Call me old-fashioned, but there's something about job security that cuts the mustard. But enough of this King Canute stuff: the tide has turned and perhaps the best thing we can all do is to get used to it, learning how to adapt and react.

Then again, that's easier said than done. Take Sarah, a friend of mine who works for a sizeable American-owned company. She's the UK managing director and regularly clocks up over a hundred hours a week. Get this: she's married too, with a daughter. Talk about pressure. I'm not saying this is for everyone – and it only works for Sarah and her family as they feel like they're in it together – but the days of the 37-hour week seem to have rented space alongside scheduled tea breaks, dinner dances and Radio Luxembourg. As corporate success becomes increasingly judged by profitability and profitability alone, so does the pressure for results increase. And if someone on the board is shouting for results, you can bet that it's you or me who has to stay back later to deliver. The Compete To Win ethos of the market economy may have opened a fair few doors, but it's changed the face of work as we know it.

Of course, there's another whole area of pressure weighing down upon us in the workplace these days: the speed of change. Often it can seem as though skills that were learnt early on can soon become redundant. I'm not talking about Morse code here, or even about the change from paper-laden to the (allegedly) paper-free office. Instead, the situation is much more real, as anyone working in IT will tell you. Mobile messages, voicemail messages, text messages, emails, faxes, memos, journals, articles, letters, phone calls and all the rest: our time at work is increasingly subject to all manner of demands. Communication advances mean information overload, all adding to the stress levels awaiting us as we turn up at work. Research published by the Institute of Management recently suggested that the need to keep up with emails comes tenth in the league of workplace stresses and pressures, ranking higher than having a bad relationship with the boss, dealing with customer complaints and lack of influence within the company.

Of course, there are the lucky ones whose work pressure has been accompanied by sufficiently chunky salaries and bonuses, so that they have been able to give up work altogether and offer their time free of charge to a good cause. Escaping the rat race can increasingly seem like a good idea, and Voluntary Service Overseas (VSO) reported that applications from business and management professionals had increased by 61 per cent in the first half of 1999.

A 1994 survey found that one in six UK employees had been in their job for less than a year, as well as that 70 per cent of people would like to work a 40-hour week while only 30 per cent of the workforce actually do so. Shockingly, one in ten of the workforce have no annual paid leave.

Following email viruses like 'Melisa' and 'I love you', I was amused to receive the following warning about a virus . . .

There is a new virus going around called 'WORK'. If you receive any sort of 'WORK' at all, whether via email, Internet or simply handed to you by a colleague . . . DO NOT OPEN IT.

'WORK' has been circulating around offices for months and those who have been tempted to open 'WORK' or even look at 'WORK' have found that their social life is deleted and their brain ceases to function properly.

If you do encounter 'WORK' via email or are faced with any 'WORK' at all, then to purge the virus, send an email to your boss with the words 'sorry . . . I'm off to the pub'. The 'WORK' should automatically be deleted from your brain.

If you receive 'WORK' on paper-document form, simply lift the document and drag the 'WORK' to your garbage can. Put on your coat and skip to the nearest bar with two friends and order three pints of beer. After repeating this action fourteen times, you will find that 'WORK' will no longer be of any relevance to you.

Send this message to everyone in your address book. If you do not have anyone in your address book, then I'm afraid the 'WORK' virus has already corrupted your life.

A tad more amusing than the average email circular we might receive. There is a real and present danger that work and the pressure and stress of work can take over our lives.

So how can we respond to all these challenges that await us at work? What should – or can – we do about it all? First up, I'm convinced that we need to recognise the difference between pressure and stress. Of itself, work pressure is not necessarily a bad thing, and for many of us it is a vital ingredient to aid increased performance. However, when it becomes too much (a definition that can only be offered by the person under pressure), it gets stressful and can start to eat in on our performance at work. For some people having a looming deadline will focus their minds and help them produce their best work, while for others it will decrease their productivity as stress and worry take over.

And what happens to us when Captain Stress takes over? From sleeplessness to loss of appetite, inability to relax to ulcers and muscle tensions, our bodies send out the signal that we are suffering. I can remember going through a particularly stressful period a few years back and developing a nasty cough. The doctor could do nothing for it, and it was only when the stress passed that I started to get better. The fact that many health problems find their roots in stress is nothing new, although it has only been fairly recently that GP surgeries have acted on this by employing counsellors to work through some of the background issues facing people.

## A vocation, not a job
But there's something more to work than finding a way to cope with all this grief. There's another treasure hunt going on – one that we're all taking part in – that offers a far greater prize than simply a decent night's sleep or a swollen salary cheque. What we need to do is to discover a sense of vocation. Instead of our work being simply a means of earning to survive, finding our vocation will allow us to view the 9-to-5 as something that is of value, that forms

part of the picture of things we consider are important in life.

The now-deceased film director Stanley Kubrick has long been one of those people to namecheck, especially if you happen to be an up-and-coming gritty actor. Edward Norton dropped in a nice little reference when being interviewed by *The Face* about his attitude towards his own work:

> It's like the thing Kubrick's supposed to have said: someone asked him, 'Why don't you take a vacation in between shooting and editing?' He said, 'That's like asking a kid to take a vacation from playing.' That's kind of how I feel about it. It doesn't feel so much like work to me.

That's what a vocation is: something that allows us to view work as relevant, even enjoyable. It blurs the edges between work and leisure, captivating us with a sense of purpose.

So that's all very well and good – especially if you feel as though you've found your vocation. But what of the rest of us, the ones left working just to earn, the ones for whom work is not fun, relevant or stimulating, but for whom it's the best that's on offer – better at least than the New Deal? What then: do we just sit back and take it?

### All work has worth
Step one, we need to change the lens. All too often we find ourselves captivated by the verdant lawn on the other side, considering our own patch to be nothing more than a scraggy dust-bowl. While this might be true enough of our

gardening abilities, when it comes to work the attitude is both unhelpful and incorrect. Here's what Paul had to say about it:'Whatever you do, work at it with all your heart, as working for the Lord, not for men' (Colossians 3:23).

If that's God's take on our work – as left-field praise and worship – then doesn't that imply that we might do well to reassess our view of what is and what is not 'good' work? OK, so it might be easier for someone working in the public sector – say a nurse or a teacher – to consider that their job has inherent worth. All they have to do is look at the smiling faces of the hordes of grateful people they help each day. But what about the bankers, the shop-workers or the machinists? What worth can be found among the sweat and the oil or the pink paper and champagne? We Christians can often find it easy to see the value in the caring professions, but struggle to declare it in many of the other employment sectors.

While I was in a developing country recently I was overwhelmed by the sense of self-esteem that was so highly visible among the people I met. Having spoken with them I was convinced that much of it came from the fact that they viewed their work – whatever it may have been – as something to be proud of. There was no question as to whether their work had value; it was plain for all to see. Yet I was confused; how can it be so clear that one type of work is of worth in one part of the world, yet that same job be considered by many Christians to be way down the list of godly professions back in the West? What's more, I was struck by just how unusual it was to find people truly believing in their work. Back home, many people I know clock-watch to some extent, and if we're honest, wouldn't most of us rather be on a three- or a four-day week so long as the money stayed the same?

*Patch Adams*, the 1998 film with Robin Williams, tells the true story of a man reacting against the mechanistic hospital environment that treated the patients as objects rather than human beings. It was a moving film, and as it drew to a close the following words filled the screen:

> During the next twelve years, Patch Adams opened a home-based family medical practice and treated more than 15,000 people without payment, malpractice insurance or formal facilities. He purchased the 105 acres in West Virginia, and construction of the Gesundheit Hospital is currently underway. To date, a waiting list of over 1,000 physicians have offered to leave their current practices and join Patch's cause.

This is what happens when someone discovers a sense of worth and value within their work, when it goes beyond merely doing a job.

I'm always challenged by Celtic Christianity, in particular by the way in which it adopts a holistic view to life. Far from separating 'church' from 'work', 'spirituality' from 'normality', it seems to be able to integrate things on a far greater level than we can, as this prayer indicates: 'The world gives itself to incessant activity merely because it knows of nothing better. The inspired man works among its whirring wheels also, but he knows whither the wheels are going. For he has found the centre where all is stillness' (from

*Celtic Daily Prayer*). Much of Celtic spirituality exudes a relationship with God in all aspects of our life and work.

One of the keys to gaining a sense of inherent value and worth within our work is self-awareness. This is a fact that has been widely recognised by the popularity of personality tests (such as Myers–Briggs), tests which, instead of claiming one type is better than another, explain that there is a plethora of personality types, each with different tendencies and leanings. It kind of makes sense to me that the better we understand our personalities, the better able we will be to express ourselves through meaningful work. By understanding our own energies and talents, we unlock the door to a whole new world of work.

A friend describes talents as 'something that we cannot help but do', and I'm convinced that if we can get ours to coincide with work then we will have made a significant step along the way to discovering our vocation. No training department can put in what God has left out.

## Colouring in

The second key to discovering a vocation is intricately bound up with the idea of how we view the workplace. I reckon that it's absolutely vital that we consider it as a place that desperately needs to be coloured and flavoured by God. Remember what Jesus said about his followers being the salt of the earth? He went on to explain that once it has lost its saltiness, salt can never regain it, and 'it is no longer good for anything, except to be thrown out and trampled by men'. As Christians we need to take seriously the work environment into which God has placed us, seeing ourselves not as ex-salty salt, but as full-on, wince-when-you-lick-it, salty-flavoured salt.

I remember not being particularly impressed by the film *Pleasantville* – I can't recall why now – but there was something about it which caught my imagination. As the enlightened saviours from the 1990s return to the monochrome repression of the 1950s, so they manage to spread their free thinking among a conservative populace. Not very good, but the way the film introduced colour got me thinking about the workplace: forget the film's message for a moment, but isn't colouring our environment what we're supposed to be doing? Aren't we supposed to be making the difference?

I know someone who recently made one of those classic email mistakes. You know the sort, an inappropriate gag that was supposed to be shared with a trusted work colleague. Instead – and thanks to the wonders of that 'Reply All' button – the wrong person got hold of my mate's precise opinion of one of their main contractors.

You can guess the rest, but suffice it to say that my techno chum wound up in front of a disciplinary board, none too chuffed at having an ear-bashing from a partner in the company of one of their best contractors. Scary stuff, and my friend ended up with a written warning in his personnel file.

A couple of weeks later he was delighted, as his manager had told him how impressed he had been with my friend's reaction to the hearing. Instead of getting bitter, angry and resentful, he had been the epitome of gracious responsibility, and had come out of the situation with increased workplace respect. OK, so as a strategy there are probably less risky ones, but it goes to show that being truly Christian in the office can make a real difference.

There's a lot of chat these days about something called Organisational Culture. This is not to do with bulk discounts to visit the Tate Modern but, as Margaret Wheatly, a management consultant, writes, 'For several years now leaders have been encouraged to consider the impact of non-material forces on organisations; culture, values, vision, ethics. Each of these concepts describes a quality of organisational life that can be observed in behaviour but doesn't exist anywhere independent of those behaviours.'

I believe that Christians who are up for influencing their working environment can alter the DNA of their employees and employers simply by following Christ's lead. After all, if we haven't got something to say about culture, values, vision or ethics, have we really grasped what Christianity is all about? And as Margaret Wheatly points out, where better to get to work influencing those factors than in the behaviour we exhibit in the workplace? Want it plain and simple? Walk the talk.

But as we know, experiences will vary from employer to employer. Some can be oppressive, squashing freedom of thought and creativity, while others will draw motivation, skills and talents out of workers. These empowering roles are plum jobs, up for grabs, and there's no reason why Christians shouldn't be at the front of the queue. What better way to express one's faith and further the kingdom than by being the sort of manager or team leader who draws out many of the good things that lie inside those they are responsible for? Isn't that basic application what faith in action is all about?

## Kingdom conduit

The third step evolves the argument, laying down the idea that, to fully appreciate our vocation, we need to consider that our profession can be a potential conduit for the kingdom of God. I don't just mean that it can hide the 36-amp wires of faith under the plaster cornice of culture (for all those DIYers of you out there): it can be a channel for God's heavenly agenda. The more theologically attuned talk about the gathered Church being the primary agent of the kingdom – or to put it another way, the community of God is the main means of seeing his dynamic presence in the here and now. In developing a decent Christian work ethic, I believe that each profession can be an agent for the kingdom of God. Through work can come God. Simple.

Jesus prayed – and we have copied – that God's kingdom would come, that his will would be done here on earth just as it happens in heaven. I'm convinced that Jesus wasn't just thinking about things being done God's way only in the bits of earth we most easily think of as sanctified, in the temples and the religious communities. God wants his will to be done in all aspects of the job market, from nursing to politics, teaching to commerce, manufacturing to research. But, of course, this can only happen once we realise that our whole profession can become fair game for God's mission.

The *Observer* in 1999 ran this piece:

Militant Christians and their fuzzier cousins in the New
Age movement are storming corporate America in a
nation-wide effort to bring God into the workplace –
and they are succeeding.

A Spiritual Audit of Corporate America, carried
out by consultant Elizabeth Denton and Professor Ian
Mitroff of the University of California Business School,
found that 60 per cent had positive views of spirituality
but not of organised religion, and 30 per cent were
positive about both. This amounts to a staggering 90 per
cent prepared to look favourably on some form of
transcendent experience involving faith.

Evidence suggests that spiritual programmes at work,
and encouraging staff not to 'leave their religion at home',
result in a happier workforce and improved production.

*Observer*, 28 November 1999

If that sort of research is being carried out, showing that
people perform better in their jobs if their spiritual dimension is first carried and second allowed through the office
doors, then the potential is certainly quite exciting. What's
more, this sort of approach to work is not merely limited
to the States; a friend of mine in the UK has recently taken
on the job of executive coach to one of the high street's
largest conglomerates. We're not talking abs and biceps here,
but helping these powerful men and women discover 'the
image of Christ they were made to be'. He won't be
ramming scripture down their throats, but he certainly is
helping to advance the kingdom of God.

One of my concerns for the next generation has been

the number of Christians who graduate from university and lose their Christian faith as they establish themselves in the workplace. The challenges facing a young adult moving into a graduate job are numerous – moving to a location where you may not know anyone, getting your feet under the table with the job, sussing out your boss, getting to know your colleagues, sorting out some leisure pursuits, making new friends, finding a first home to rent or buy, keeping up with family and friends. Finding a new Christian community is on the list of stuff that needs to be sorted out, but there are a few other things that understandably need your attention first. So when you do check a few out, can you find one in which you can worship and which will equip you to live as a Christian in the new world in which you find yourself? The life transition from uni to workplace is a challenge for anyone. Even those who have been the most zealous of Christians during their university years stumble in their faith making this significant transition. As just one example, one figure which has been thrown around is that over 50 per cent of university CU presidents are nowhere with God within three years of graduating. This situation is tragic. For a number of years I've been wanting to make a contribution to this need, so I was thrilled that Joshua Generation has been able to appoint a team member to respond to this situation. Our workplace guy is now working to support young adults through developing holistic discipleship resources, networking people together for peer support and mentoring, and liaising with churches to develop ministries in these areas.

## Expectation

There's a story – certainly one of those urban myths that deal more in meaning than historical truth – about a school that was going through some difficult times. The head called three teachers into her office, explaining that in an effort to improve the grades they were (for one term only) siphoning off the three best teachers in the school and placing them each in charge of a class made up of the *crème de la crème* of students.

The term went by, and the experiment took place with no one but the head and the three teachers knowing anything about it. At the end of it the head called the three into her study and congratulated them on an astounding string of results. Each student had improved significantly, and the amount of effort being put into the lessons by the teachers themselves had been equally improved. There were, the head told them, just two things that she had kept to herself at the start of the term. First, the teachers had not been given the best children in the school. In fact they were made up of randomly selected pupils, completely varied in ability. The difference was that the teachers believed that the pupils were the best in the school. Second, she broke the news that neither were they the three best teachers in the school. For one term, though, all three believed that they were at the top of the pile, and that is what made the difference.

Expectation can make a huge difference, not just to our attitudes but consequently to our output and performance as well. The truth is that we seldom exceed our expectations: if we aim at nothing we'll probably hit it. As Henry Ford (of motor car fame) so wisely put it, 'Whether you think you can or whether you think you can't, you're probably right.'

Sitting on a train from London to Yorkshire I was surprised to hear an announcement over the intercom, just minutes after we pulled out of King's Cross. We were told that the journey would take 'approximately' three hours, and the train manager went to great pains to stress that this was only an approximate figure. Within half an hour we had received numerous messages detailing our progress and reminding us that it was only an estimated time of arrival. Sure enough, we were late.

I don't know what you think about self-fulfilling prophecies, but in our working environment I'm convinced that we have the power to talk ourselves to some of the farthest reaches of success or failure. After all, athletes know this, and many times has it been claimed that 80 per cent of the outcome is determined by psychological factors.

While we may seldom exceed our expectations, God on the other hand plays a different game. He frequently exceeds our expectations, as Paul was keen to point out when he wrote to the church at Ephesus: 'Now to him who is able to do immeasurably more than all we ask or imagine, according to his power that is at work within us' (Ephesians 3:20).

God can do more than we could ever dream, hope or expect. Why? Because of the work being carried out by the Holy Spirit within us.

I'm always wowed by the story of Joseph, even to the extent of tapping away to Lord Lloyd Webber's version of the tale. You probably know the story: fancy coat, big dreams, slavery, prison, interpretation, success. Eventually he lands the top job: Prime Minister of Egypt. You'd have thought that getting to be PM would have been the career high, but it gets better. His brothers turn up during the seven-year famine and ask for assistance. Once he has revealed his identity and the brothers are feeling more than slightly guilty about selling him to the traders all those years before, Joseph delivers his line: 'You intended to harm me, but God intended it for good to accomplish what is now being done, the saving of many lives' (Genesis 50:20).

Joseph's destiny was not just to sit on a decent pile of grain, but to continue the covenant that God had made with his people Israel. By being in Egypt at that strategic time to manage the strong economy, he was able to provide for both Egypt and God's people when they were weak. Talk about exceeding his expectations! God seems to have done pretty well there – trumping PM with the role of deliverer of his own people.

I know from my own life that – even though they might not be in quite the same league as Joseph's – God has frequently exceeded my expectations. When I was at school I was in remedial English and struggled with many of the basics. I never would have thought that God would have been able to use my working life; but somewhere along the way I've managed to pick up a couple of degrees and write a couple of books, and my world continues to expand.

So that all sounds nice enough, but unfortunately bad things do happen to good people. Instead of burying our heads in the sand here I believe that we need to get real about things. We will all taste failure at some point, and it can be tough not to let that crush our sense of expectation. I know people who have applied for fifty or sixty jobs and not got any of them. I've known people who have had great relationships with their boyfriends or girlfriends – relationships which have filled them with self-confidence – only to find themselves struggling to keep it together when the relationship has eventually ended. Those sorts of knocks are hard to bounce back from.

As evolving creatures, many of us reach for the mental To Do list as soon as we've had a brush with disappointment. 'Never Trust Anyone Ever Again' goes the entry and, of course, that is one way of avoiding disappointment. Then again, so is migrating to Skegness.

However, I believe that God is in the business of restoring expectation to us. As the prophet Joel told his peers, 'I will repay you for the years the locusts have eaten' (Joel 2:25), and that is precisely what God is capable of doing 2,500 years later.

Graduating from vicar factory was a tricky period for me. I was coming to the conclusion that my years in training had been a waste of time, that my faith had wound up undermined and people had tried to make me someone I wasn't. Why hadn't I gone to a different Bible college instead? In truth they weren't such bad years after all, as I can look back now and see that God used them as part of the continuing work of him shaping and moulding me. What I did know then was that I felt God promised to restore the years that the locust had eaten.

I have a friend who faced bankruptcy and lost everything:

wife, company, home, money. He lived through years of brokenness and pain, and now he's in an altogether happier place: married with a child and a new home and company. Of course, that's not to say that any pain we go through is an early warning sign of phenomenal success, wealth and happiness due to land on us later on. For every one story of a rich Christian there are a dozen that show poor ones. Does that mean God likes them less? Of course not – and I don't want to push some kind Prosperity Gospel here (i.e. God rewards faith with cash) – but it is true to say that God does restore. It might not be what we had in mind, but God's idea of success is way beyond our own. It's said that it takes twelve positive experiences to make up for one negative one. When God's involved, I'm sure that equation doesn't bother him in the slightest.

If you want something that you've never had before, the chances are that you'll have to do something that you've never done before. After all, the Bible tells us that 'faith is being sure of what we hope for and certain of what we do not see' (Hebrews 11:1). So it makes sense to me that we need to reach out with our careers to grab hold of the things which we're keen for. Picturing where we believe God is asking us to go in our careers, visualising the things he would have us do, are ways of transforming the job into the vocation. Call it the power of positive thinking or mere daydreaming – whatever – ponder, pray and get in the habit of expecting God to do great things: it works.

Now there's a lot of chat going round about mentoring – the process of spending time with someone you admire and respect in order that some of their good stuff might rub off on you, that their encouragement and wisdom might help you achieve your goals. Much of the chat that's been going on has delivered eight-point plans for effective mentoring, offering tips and timetables to better scale the mentoring mountain. A lot of it is rhetoric, and the reality is that I'm not so sure about making such a precise science out of it; at the heart I'm convinced that it's about (as Proverbs says) 'iron sharpening iron', or one person coming alongside and helping another out with their talents and skills. It happens naturally, and needing it is part of our genetic make-up.

There's a film called *The Muse*. Taking its nod from Greek mythology (where muses – angelic beings – inspired creativity), the film follows a struggling Hollywood script-writer whose career is going nowhere fast, until the day a friend introduces him to – you guessed it – the muse. She moves in with his family, and not only does he manage to write an awesome film script but his wife starts a cookie business, selling bucket-loads to topnotch eateries. But, of course, there is trouble in paradise, and one day two people visit who explain their search for a missing patient from their local psychiatric hospital. They tell the scriptwriter how the patient has done a bunk and is often to be found trying to convince people that she is someone else. Well, of course, you can imagine the shock, and Mr and Mrs ride the film out with some serious questions on their mind: were they duped, was the muse a fake, would the same events have transpired had they known of her history? One thing's for sure, though: the muse changed their expectation and released their talent.

Once a month I meet up with Paul, one of my good friends – I'd describe him as one of my mentors. We eat and we talk, and not so long back he told me one of the reasons he meets with me. 'Because I want to encourage you to fulfil your calling in life,' he said. I wasn't quite sure what to say back so I mumbled something about could he pass the salt, please. Later, after his words had sunk in a little, I realised just how important having someone who believes in you can be. Of course, we'll have to wait and see about how all that 'fulfilling potential' stuff works out, but I can tell you something: my expectation levels ride high.

So if it helps us to be given support and encouragement, doesn't it follow that we can do the same for others? It's not about giving someone all the answers, but simply being able to offer them time, attention and the belief that their talents are of inherent worth and value. By the way, if you're looking for an example of how to do this, who better to turn to than Jesus? He nurtured expectation in a plethora of people drawn from a wide social group, and left them better people.

### Life action
1  Make space for a time of reflection, and place something in front of you that symbolises the work you do. Carefully consider before God how he values your work and how you can develop the way you think about your work to see more in line with the way he does. Pray and ask God to use you to colour and flavour your work environment for him, and to develop your profession as a conduit for the kingdom.

2 What are some of the areas of pressure that you face in your work? Do these help you perform or do they cause you nothing but stress? How can you decrease the demands or increase the resources available to you to remove this pressure?

3 Who do you know in your profession, more senior and advanced than you, that you really respect? Arrange breakfast, lunch or an after-work drink with them on a regular basis. Ask for their advice on your personal development and introductions to people who can help you in your work – generally benefit from their experience and wisdom. If they are a Christian, pray together; perhaps if they aren't you could offer to pray for them anyway.

4 Plan some time in your diary to take a career prayer retreat somewhere you find God; it doesn't have to be somewhere mega-religious. Pray and ask God what you should be expecting in your vocation.

# 3

## *Friends and Family*

### The scene

It's not going to come as a shock to many of you to read that singleness is on the increase in the UK. It's not just due to people waiting longer to get married, either; the list of those without long-term partners includes people 'between relationships', widows and widowers, divorcees, single parents, those who are happy to live the single life and those who have chosen singleness because they struggle with their sexuality. The numbers of people living alone have caused a significant change in the building policies of many local authorities, who are now often to be found concentrating efforts on smaller apartments rather than 'family' houses. In fact, the official government forecast is that an extra 4.4 million new homes will have to be built by 2016. In 1971 one in five households were made up of single people, while in 1991 the rates had risen to one in four. By the time 2016 comes around, it is estimated that one in three will be the figure, while just four years later, in 2020, it has been suggested that four in ten will be single-person households. Today in London 40 per cent of households are made up of the more traditional families, while 57 per cent comprise single people.

Is it any wonder that loneliness is such a major problem facing our society? Even moving to be surrounded by more people – many of them in similar situations – cannot offer full immunisation from the sting of isolation. Mother Teresa commented that the greatest problem in our society is not tuberculosis or any other disease, but the sense of being alone.

For many it can feel as though even the calendar is against them, with Christmas-time topping the list of many people's Difficult Seasons. At a time where family togetherness seems to be the social norm, singleness sticks out like a sore thumb. This came home to me the other year when I received a letter that had been mailed out to all residents in my area of London, asking each of us to keep an eye out for not just the elderly, but the young and single too. With suicide rates rising around the December festive season, it was a shocking reminder of just how hard life can get for some.

Family life has changed so much over the years that now there are significant numbers within current generations of young people who are growing up part of split families. They're not the first, either, and there are currently plenty of adults out there who have no model of 'family' life, no experience of people staying together.

Recent reports have suggested that the way we approach

friendship is changing, too. Instead of maintaining close relationships with a large group of friends, we opt for intimacy with smaller numbers. We form small groups that are hard to penetrate, providing support, amusement and companionship throughout the many tides of life – life, incidentally, which seems to be imitating art (although 'art' might be stretching it a tad here), as we move more towards the Joey, Monica, Phoebe, Ross, Rachel and Chandler model. While *Friends* might be completely removed from reality in many ways, it seems to be the aspiration that many people live for.

But, of course, singleness isn't all limp sandwiches and TV guides. As a single guy myself, I can say that it has much to commend it. Also, we all need to understand the shape of society and work out the best way for us to respond. Of course, in the middle of any change, when the past is still fresh in the mind, the new can often be automatically labelled 'bad' and the old 'good'. If only life were ever that simple.

The chapter before last on Identity and Image looked at the core of our worth, perhaps enabling us not to feel lonely when we're alone or in a crowd. We'll be moving on to relationships and sexuality in the next, where among other issues we'll hopefully find some resources for keeping us from being lonely in marriage. This chapter, however, aims to give some clues as to how we can invest in friends and family.

## Friends

Without friendship, there is no Bible. From beginning to end the Bible is about humankind's relationship with God and with one another. It is the axis around which the whole of creation revolves. God exists within a family. OK, so it's a reasonably unusual family, but with him as Father, Son and Holy Spirit there are the definite parallels between the Trinity and the glue that holds us together with others. God is a dynamic community and we have been made in his image. That means where God thrives on relationship, so we do too. Where unity and interaction, interdependence and harmony are the norm, so too can they be found in our own emotional DNA. We need to live in community, to experience and express love. Even with our differences and distinctives we need to be around people, whether they come in the form of family, friends or a wider concept of community. The human race hungers for belonging, friendship, community and love. This fundamental truth is part of the script that is almost impossible to ignore.

So just who are our friends? Mine are the ones who know both the best and the worst about me. They are the people who I trust, the people I have learnt to be vulnerable with and who have learnt to be the same with me. They're the ones to whom I don't just reply 'fine' when asked how I am. Instead, the friendship goes beyond the superficial.

Of course, in going beyond the superficial, true friendship enters some choppy water. The early honeymoon period will inevitably be followed by one of disillusionment, to a greater or lesser extent. I found this when I offered a friend a place to stay. He was stuck and my flat was small, but he moved in and we got on just fine. In fact, it was more than just fine, it was a blast. All we needed were a couple of babes to move in next door and our *Men Behaving Badly* fantasy would have been complete. But the Lad Paradise didn't last as we eventually discovered each other's downsides. To my surprise I found out that untidiness annoyed the pants off me, and he soon got fed up with me leaving the washing up and never being at home.

I should have known what to expect, really, as this wasn't the first time I'd swallowed the bittersweet pill of the shared home. Some years previously I'd had the opportunity to live in a house with three other Christians. 'Mmmmm, taste of heaven,' I thought as I moved in. It didn't take me long to change my mind: instead of early morning praise and worship sessions followed by ritual prophetic encouragement hours, we argued about everything and nothing, from whose turn it was to do the shopping to whose turn it was to clean the toilet. It was a tad disappointing and certainly brought an element of realism to the concept of Christian community. Still, it taught me many valuable lessons, and I've learnt how to de-flea even the largest of rugs.

If you're looking for a fully functioning classic example of biblical friendship, you couldn't do much better than to look at the relationship between Jesus and John the Dunker (Baptist). They were different; John was the archetypal wailing weirdo (perhaps we're stretching things a little with this one), eating locusts and honey and living in the desert, while Jesus was part of a good Jewish family, with a nice trade under his belt. Yet there was a respect and affirmation between them, as we can see throughout the Gospel accounts of their encounters. John famously said of Jesus that 'he must become greater; I must become less' (John 3:30), and indeed he did (about one head's worth less, to be precise).

There's something important about the differences between friends. We may concentrate on the areas of common ground and similarity between us, but I wonder whether what really makes a friendship is the differences between people and the influence they have. This certainly is the case with my friend Paulie (a term of affection) and me. On the surface we're very similar: same age, same tastes, similar degree of ambition; but in many other ways – particularly temperament – we're very different. Often his way of doing things will be completely different to mine, but where with other friends this might push us apart, we have learnt to make it work for a better relationship. I learn from him and he from me, often resulting in compromise and preferment.

There are occasions, however, when we find out things about friends that we simply don't like. We can go off people and at times like this – perhaps as a friendship nears the end of its natural life – it can be tempting to create a distorted image of the person in our minds. Instead of seeing them as a combination of the good that once attracted us and the newly discovered bad, we block out the good, discarding it as it no longer fits with our revised interpretation of the soon-to-be ex-friend's character. This all might sound a little on the cynical side, but I know it's not just me who has experienced both sides of this saddening phenomenon.

## Family

We all know that family life is one of the biggest challenges facing us. Not only does it test our nerve, patience and all-round saintliness, but it can end up costing us almost everything we have. The challenges face us all: even if we have no contact with our natural family the absence will undoubtedly have an effect.

A friend of mine is the son of a preacher. His dad led a large church in which the family grew up, and one day the role of church leader was passed down from father to son. It was difficult for the father to stand back and watch his son take the church in fresh directions, difficult to see him do things in ways that he never would have done. But the father did stand back and allow his son to march to the beat of his own drum, and all in all it was the very model of good family relationships.

A while later the son's own son returned home one day wearing a friend's Arsenal shirt. Nothing unusual about that, you may think, but my friend had been a Liverpool supporter since he could talk. More than that, his wife had been a fan, too, and so had his children. Greeted with the sight of his son in such disloyal colours, he got quite irate and sent him to his room with the order to change into something more 'family conscious', like the 1983 Liverpool away strip. As the young Gunners fan disappeared beyond the top of the stairs, my friend's wife turned to him and spoke razor-sharp truth (perhaps a good reason not to have a wife, I've always thought): 'It's a good job your dad didn't handle you like that when you first took over the church.'

Of course, his wife was right, and it's a challenge that

faces us all. We can so easily become blinded by the intensity of passion whenever family matters are in play. Logic, clear-headed thought and objectivity can go out the window as the pain of 'how could you do that to me?' takes over. It's a common challenge to us all for another reason, too: children will by their nature do things differently to their parents. Part of growing up from childhood dependence involves moving through a period of independence, making rebellion an essential part of emotional development. If we cannot kick against the identity formed for us by our parents, how then can we establish our own? In fact, there's a theory commonly held by therapists that parents don't need to be perfect: they simply need to be 'good enough'. If the parent does nothing wrong, how can the child ever move on from their position of dependence and unquestioning acceptance? If, however, the parent is good enough, the child will see enough flaws and failings to break away, yet there will have been enough unconditional understanding to provide a strong foundation.

After his wife gave my friend a little helping hand in seeing what was going on, he went out and bought his son the whole Arsenal strip. He may have felt like the most terrible father in the world – encouraging his son to follow so shallow a team – but something tells me he was good enough.

Try as you might, there's no way that a family can function to the best of its ability without offering conditional love. For it to work, the love has to be the unconditional variety, and if I didn't know this already I got a firm reminder one year when I was preaching in Malta. At the end of the meeting, after the prayer session had wound up, a man came up to me and asked to have a chat. He was slightly older than me and was full of encouraging things to tell me. I was dead chuffed and fully appreciated his kindness. Then it went pear-shaped. He told me that he had one problem with the way I did things, and that it was located in my left ear. He told me how his own son not only wears an earring, but that he repeatedly comes home with additional bits of his body pierced. Father had laid down the law to the son, but to no avail. It had reached crisis point and he had recently delivered an ultimatum: one more piercing and you're out. It was not surprising that he didn't particularly like male preachers – or any other males, for that matter – wearing earrings. It seemed pretty clear to me that he was facing a choice: either he kept his relationship with his son by giving unconditional love, or he lost it by drawing a line in the sand. The decision, as they say, was his.

I was at a conference some time later describing the culture of the current generation of twentysomethings. A man stood up at the end and said that, as a father, the description had rung bells in his mind, describing exactly how his son ticked. He explained how they had nothing in common, but the only reason they got on was the fact that they loved each other. He'd hit the nail on the head with that one: it is the power of love that transcends all manner of barriers.

For a long time we've understood family to mean Mum, Dad, a couple of kids, an estate car for Pops, a smaller vehicle for the wifey, holidays with smiles, and a dribbling Granny visiting at Christmas and Easter. With the growth of single households and the rise in the numbers of single people, this is becoming an increasingly irrelevant picture. As society changes, so too will our definition be forced to change; instead of being the couple plus 2.4 children we will have to encompass the slightly more abstract idea of household and beyond as defining what family is.

Take me, for example. I consider that the people I work with are actually part of my family; we're really close to each other, supportive of each other and love each other. Or there are some friends I have who happen to have a large house. They've decided to open it up to all sorts of people (and I'm not talking about Sunday visitors here), so it's pretty usual for them to have ten people staying with them at any one time. They aren't just passing through, either. In fact, it's an offer of much more than just accommodation, as they go beyond guests and become part of a family, a living, dynamic and vibrant community.

Another test facing families is how parents cope when the children leave home. For many, the kids are the glue, the common purpose that Mum and Dad share. Exit kids, and it's not uncommon to witness all manner of changes going on within the couple's relationship as they try to redefine their identity. Some don't make it through the challenge of rebuilding their friendship, and it can be a time when many decide to separate, unable to reconcile the differences that now appear so stark.

The Bible offers many examples of family life, but there aren't many that expose the complexities of familial jealousy quite as well as – yup, it's my favourite again – the story of

Joseph. Getting sold into slavery by his brothers over a few unwise comments was a fairly poor turn of events, but the problems of parental favouritism are still around today. Likewise the quiet jealousy of the hard-done-by sibling, as described in the story of the Prodigal Son. While his ex-pig-tending brother enjoys the best of his father's table, the brother is left feeling out of place and jealous. It's a wonderful picture of the unconditional love offered by our Father in heaven, but it also exposes our own insecurities. We can all feel pangs of envy as others get the prize we desire, and often the roots can be found in our own insecurity. In Luke 15, the at-home brother's problems seem to come from his not knowing that he was loved just as much by his father all along. At any time, he is told, he could have enjoyed a similar feast, yet his assumptions had told him otherwise.

Thankfully, while these New and Old Testament stories present an accurate picture of family strife, God has got other plans. He longs for restoration and is more than able to deliver. He longs for reconciliation between parents and children, just as he does between friends. It's a heart-warming thought, and as the Pentecostals are fond of saying, HE IS ABLE! Amen to that.

### Life action

1   Who are the most important friends in your life? When you next see them or chat on the telephone, tell them how much they mean to you. It might be as simple as saying, 'I am really thankful that you are my friend.'

2   How can you show hospitality to someone you know –

and not just the usual person that you might invite round for dinner, but someone who would be really blessed if you asked them over for a meal?

3  Have you ever thought of expanding your household? Have you got a spare room you could rent to a friend or someone in need? Don't use the excuse that it's your guest room – be honest, how often do you have guests to stay? For the amount of times that you do, surely you or they could sleep on the sofa! You might even be in the position where you could buy a bigger home in order to expand.

4  Do you have any strained family relationship/s? If so, what could you do this week to show generosity and grace in it? Now stop faffing around: just do it. Take the initiative – pop in, make a phone call, write a letter. If relationships in your family are great, then why not do something generous for no reason other than appreciation?

# *4*
# *Relationships and Sexuality*

## The scene

In an interview with *The Face*, that most un-Britney-like of pop queens, Macy Gray, was asked about sex. 'Do you,' enquired the interviewer, 'go completely mad when you haven't had sex for ages?' Quite what it had to do with the price of bread I'm not sure, but our Macy played by the rules and replied with the required headline-fuelling mix of honesty and 'liberty': 'Hmmmm. I don't really go that long without it too often!'

When asked who the people might be that she doesn't go too long without 'hmmmmm'ing, Macy replies: 'There's a couple of guys that I hang out with. When I'm in town or something.'

But how, asked the quivering journo, do you cope

emotionally with having more than one casual sexual partner on the go at any one time?

> Um. As long as you're safe and you're honest about it, it's not gonna mess with your head. It's just sex, y'know? I learned a long time ago you can be emotionally involved with someone and then have sex – but you shouldn't get emotionally involved with someone because you have sex. The most you can hope for is that you'll have fun and you won't catch anything. Women are conditioned to give in to that, emotionally, but that's tradition, the past and that, and that don't make a whole lotta sense. Be aware of cause and effect and just go from there.

Macy's take on sex and relationships is a textbook example of how this kind of stuff is perceived within our culture. The restraints are off and each of us is (according to contemporary opinion) free to wander wherever our appetites take us. But there's more to it than that: why would a magazine such as *The Face* be interested in the sex life of a particular recording artist? Because it sells. Face facts, people, sex is the number one fashion accessory, the ultimate status symbol. But like all sartorial statements, this one has to be worn right. Spout off about monogamy and you'll be about as cool as a Global Hypercolor t-shirt. Multiple partners and an 'it's just sex' attitude on the other hand delivers a ready-to-eat slice of hot street cred to your door, easily on a par with the latest Paris and Milan 'must haves'.

But don't get the wrong impression: when it comes to fashion I can't be doing with all that 'cooler than thou' stuff. The Levis Store is more my style, and it was with a certain sense of shock that I walked away from the counter recently. I had just bought a jumper when the cashier told me to help myself from the jar by the till. Mmmm, thought I, free sweeties. I was wrong, however, as they turned out to be condoms. I'm also not really one for grabbing those prime-time evangelism opportunities, but this time I just felt like saying something, so I said no thanks and mentioned that as I was a Christian I was saving sex for my marriage partner. The cashier seemed surprised and I went on my way.

Sex has become not just another marketing tool; it really is *the* marketing tool. Not only does a glimpse of breast or hint of eroticism grab the attention like nothing else, but as with Macy and the Levis Store, it has become the litmus test by which all other cultural credentials are measured.

Lest we forget, sex is not just about having fun; it also has its links with making babies. The UK has the highest teenage pregnancy rate in Europe, and comes second in the European league of abortion rates. Birth rates among fifteen- to nineteen-year-olds were seven times those in the Netherlands, where similar numbers are having sex but are more likely to use contraception. The tide is changing with older people too, as common-law marriage – a phrase which even now seems curiously outdated – has become the norm, with people choosing to live together without tying the knot. In the 1960s 6 per cent of people chose to cohabit, while in the 1970s 33 per cent opted for it. In the 1980s the figure had risen to 58 per cent, while in the 1990s it peaked at 80 per cent.

For those who do make the commitment and decide to get married the chances of success are not guaranteed. The rate of divorce in the UK is beaten only by that in America, and for many young married couples the chances of making it through to their first few anniversaries are dangerously slim. What's more, the consequences of divorce are often hardest on the children. Some figures recently released helped paint the picture faced by many young people today: 25 per cent of those whose parents are married will divorce by the time they are sixteen; 70 per cent of children whose parents divorce are under ten years old at the time; 40 per cent of children lose all contact with their fathers within two years of divorce or separation.

In a recent survey in America, 40 per cent of women said they had been forced to have sex against their will. Horrifically, only 3 per cent of men admitted to forcing women in such a way. It's as if the culture conspires to widen the gap between men and women; women believe that they are being violated while men believe they are having fun.

Sex offending against children may be more common than previous population surveys have shown. Police crime reports indicate about 76,000 cases a year. Excluding 'flashing' incidents, 13 per cent of child molesters are relatives, 68 per cent are known to their victims and only 18 per cent are strangers. Eighty per cent of offences take place in the home of the offender or the victim, and despite a widespread belief that child sex offenders are incurable and offend frequently, reconviction rates are about 20 per cent over twenty years, whereas non-sexual offenders are reconvicted at a rate of about 50 per cent over two years. Between 60 and 70 per cent of abusers target only girls, while adolescents probably commit up to a third of child sex crimes. Finally, the emotional consequences of being abused in the home by a known and trusted adult are often more serious than being abused by a stranger.

Our times are also marked by increasing degrees of sexual confusion. It seems as though more young people wrestle with issues of identity and orientation than are prepared to admit to it, although the previous couple of decades have done much to make sexual experimentation appear both more accessible and widespread. Throughout the early 1990s I remember sporadically tuning in to Channel Four's late-night post-pub show *The Word*, the one with 'our' Terry Christian and Amanda De Cadenet. Week in and week out, the show was one long advert for bisexuality, with bi-blind date, bi-blindfold snogging and an all-round isn't-it-about-time-you-tried-it approach to all matters non-heterosexual.

Slightly more serious debate has been taking place long before and after this Friday night bi-fest graced the airwaves. People have grappled with the issue of 'nature or nurture', discussing whether we are born with a sexual identity or whether it is learnt. It seems strange to me that the Church has generally failed to face up to these questions. A friend of mine waited until he was in his late twenties before he told a Christian that he was struggling with his sexual identity. While he had been in turmoil about it for years, he knew that to come out and expose even a whiff of confusion within the Church could very well leave him isolated and ostracised. It's such a shame, especially as there are plenty of open-minded Christians about, yet still we promote a message of blanket condemnation and castigation instead of unconditional love and care.

As mentioned in the earlier chapter on Friends and Family, the number of single-person households is on the up, and added to the cultural changes and distinctives listed above, it's clear that we are experiencing a massive shift in approach to relationships and sexuality. Whether that be in divorce, abortion or teenage pregnancy rates, abuse figures or climate for sexual experimentation, the positions seem to be shifting, putting even greater distance between the established church ideas and those espoused by the likes of Macy Gray and the Levis Store.

## Sexuality

All of this brings us neatly to the question 'What is sexuality?' Clearly, with so much change going on it cannot be that sexuality is only equal to sex. No, sexuality must be about more than just sex; surely it is about the expression of our gender genes? As Christians we're then faced with two further questions: how do we express our sexuality, and how do we express sex?

In his best-seller *Men are from Mars, Women are from Venus*, John Gray describes an imaginary occurrence between the inhabitants of two different planets. The Martians get along just fine with the Venusians, but it all turns sour when they decide to fly to Earth. Gray imagines that something goes wrong as they pass through the atmosphere, after which they wake up with selective amnesia. From that moment on, says the author, 'men and women have been in conflict'.

*Men are from Mars, Women are from Venus* makes some crass generalisations and wades happily into the bog of gender stereotyping, but it does at least highlight the need for us as individuals to recognise the differences in people around us – regardless of gender. It is vital that we work towards understanding, taking differences into account and searching for answers as to why our behaviour is as it is. Given that sexuality isn't just for sex, we need to be able to have good friendships which don't involve sex.

It's time to return to that question of how we might go about expressing our sexuality. The truth is that sexuality finds expression in all manner of outlets: through feelings, friendships, laughter, tears, home, clothes, sport, interests and communication. I often get comments from people visiting my flat for the first time, asking me who helped me decorate. People usually assume that my mother or a girlfriend has picked out the colours, but it's something that I've done myself. You see, we're so shackled by generalisations that we are surprised when a bloke likes flowers or when a woman works on cars. It's kind of embarrassing that we still live in this *Carry On* universe, but it's true; we don't expect people to express their identity in ways other than the generally narrow preconceptions of good male and female behaviour.

## Sexual intimacy

Of course, it's important for the Church to work things out on this topic. After all, if we're agreeing with the rest of the culture that sexuality is expressed through sexual intercourse as well as telling people not to have sex before marriage, that does seem to leave single people in a bit of a sexual desert. Instead, we need to find the truth, to come up with responses, and in so doing to find the true importance of sexual intimacy.

Let's jump forward first and deal with that messy sexual intimacy bit. Christians believe that the best context in which people can enjoy (note that word) sex is in a life-long committed relationship. As it says in Genesis 2:24, 'For this reason a man will leave his father and mother and be united to his wife, and they will become one flesh.' So we see that the context within which sex should – according to the Bible – be expressed is between one man and one woman within a life-long relationship. In our Western society we've defined and expressed this one woman/man relationship through the institution of marriage, a public ceremony where promises are made before God and wit-nesses that the two will be faithful. Sometimes as Christians we have a tendency to make the ceremony sacred rather than the life-long relationship, forgetting that the ceremony is a cultural phenomenon.

Interestingly enough, a recent piece in *The Times* added a new twist to the argument: it claimed that one in three American schools teaches that abstaining from sexual intercourse is the only appropriate way to behave, as lessons on birth control are increasingly outlawed within the educational system. Teachings that were once the mainstay of far-right religious groups are marching quickly on towards becoming the norm in schools that may traditionally have resisted the rhetoric of the Bible belt. The report went on to say that

> a survey of head teachers found that 34 per cent of schools taught that not only was abstinence preferred, but that it was the proper form of behaviour. A study of superintendents of school districts found that 35 per cent had policies which dictated that abstinence should be taught as the only option for teenagers.

Not only is it more popular to teach abstinence from sexual intercourse before marriage, but it has also been proved that marriage is the best framework within which to bring up children. Some estimates suggest that almost 50 per cent of cohabiting couples who have children will split up by the time their child is one year old: this compares to 8 per cent of married parents. However, as mentioned earlier, marriage is by no means fireproof, and UK divorce rates remain alarmingly high. But more than being a safer bet or a nice day out, marriage is also the ultimate expression of loving commitment. 'For richer, for poorer, for better or for worse, in sickness and in health': when my time comes to say the words, I know I'll mean them for real and will be in it for life.

## Singleness and beyond

So if that is God's take on how sex is best expressed, what about those of us who are single? How do single people wrestle with these issues? Of course we share the natural desire for companionship with the rest of the human race, and after all, wasn't it God himself who pondered that it is not good for people to be alone? Companionship is top of the list of our 'must haves', not just this season but from the dawn of time itself. We're more than just animals; we need interdependence to thrive.

As a single person I know how important it is to make sure that our very human needs are met. Personally, I have a real need for companionship when I get in from work. Where my married friends can lean on each other, if I hadn't made sure things were different I could be left with nothing but the amusingly shaped tea cosy to pour out my soul with. Instead, I know there are friends I can telephone at (almost) any time, day or night, to off-load with and generally satiate my appetite for support. Likewise there are friends who will call me to talk things through with, friends who know I'll provide a listening ear. I have plenty of people come to stay, and even though I live alone it hardly feels like it. Good planning for holidays, regular meals out and plenty of home-spun hospitality seems to all go well into the mix, and right now singleness is a complete blessing rather than a ticking clock that I just can't wait to speed along. In fact, being single means that I can have a greater number of meaningful friendships than would be possible or perhaps appropriate were I married.

There's a whole bag full of other issues lying in wait for the single person, from holidays to entertainment, future plans to immediate needs. Each needs to be addressed, and while the rest of the world seems to be coping just fine with it, I've got a sneaking feeling that the Western world's preference for marriage as the ideal state means that we gloss over issues that are particularly pertinent to those of us without partners.

But if there's a natural desire for companionship there's an equally potent desire for sexual intimacy. You only have to sit through a couple of Hollywood's finest movies to figure this one out. *American Pie* took the declaration of this position to new heights, with randiness so strong that it led to the most unnatural union of boy with cake. Mmmmmm, not tasty. But while Kevin Spacey's character in *American Beauty* may not have been hanging around the patisserie section of his local deli with a glazed look on his face, it did show how that basic sexual desire stays close by on our journey throughout life. And a good thing too; there's nothing wrong with sex and I hope to be at it well into my twilight years. But cherry pies and girls the age of your daughter? No thanks.

Third, there's also a natural desire for people to have children. For women there's the added pressure that comes from the ticking of the biological clock. I've spoken to plenty of single women worried about the increased risks to mother and baby as they advance through their thirties and beyond. Men may be free from the immediate worries about age, but the desire to pass on genes and a whole lot more is still strong within them. A number of single women I know choose to meet some of their desires by spending time among families with young children. You could say that this is a fairly unsatisfactory position, that it's a small consolation, but many of them have found it to be a happy compromise between present situation and future desire, not to mention the huge support it is to often over-stretched young families.

These three natural desires are the key players that draw us into marriage: companionship, sexual intimacy and children. As the Apostle Paul wrote, however, there are great advantages to being single:

> I would like you to be free from concern. An unmarried man is concerned about the Lord's affairs – how he can please the Lord. But a married man is concerned about the affairs of this world – how he can please his wife – and his interests are divided. An unmarried woman or virgin is concerned about the Lord's affairs: Her aim is to be devoted to the Lord in both body and spirit. But a married woman is concerned about the affairs of this world – how she can please her husband. I am saying this for your own good, not to restrict you, but that you may live in a right way in undivided devotion to the Lord.
>
> 1 Corinthians 7:32–5

There are huge advantages to being single, one of the greatest being, as Paul points out, an undivided heart with which to serve God. It's obvious that being single means that you're able to commit far more time to other things. Of course, this is a double-sided coin and there is a danger that in becoming too focused on work we slip into the territory of the workaholic. Dangerous ground, this, and having seen friends struggle with it, I'd say it can be fairly hard to break out of.

It seems to me that a lot of single people are like passengers sitting on a plane waiting for take-off. They're holding up the plane insisting there is another passenger to arrive. It seems as if many of us single people sit on the runway of life waiting for our life-long partner to come along before we allow the flight to take off. Personally I'm convinced that God wants us to live life to the full in the here and now. Singleness is not the stage before marriage or a second-rate social status. We need to fly now, and if we are to be married we'll discover that our partner is already on the plane going towards the same destination.

It sounds like a silly example, but I can remember talking to a person who was bemoaning the state of their crockery, how nothing matched and it was all chipped. They'd seen a set they liked and they could afford it, but something was holding them back. In their mind they'd always thought that a nice dinner service was something they'd put on their wedding list, so they were 'making do' until then. With no one on the scene it looked like being a long wait. It struck me as a real shame that they considered themselves unworthy because of their marital state. Following our conversation they went out and purchased a complete dinner service, despite the lack of ring on fourth finger.

But what if you do want to find the right person? What if a life of singleness stretching into the future isn't quite your cup of tea? Some Christians think that there is only one 'right' partner out there for you. If you manage to marry that person then you're in God's will; however, if you don't make the right choice then you're asking for trouble. The problem with this view is one of logic: if one person marries the 'wrong' partner – and all proponents of this view would admit that this happens – then that means there are two other people out there who have missed their 'right' partner. If they've missed out, then there are some more people out there who've got it wrong, and so the story goes until you conclude that this way, everyone ends up with the wrong partner simply because of that original poor choice. It just doesn't make sense, and I have to admit that I take a different view of things. I'm convinced that instead of us looking for God's chosen partner, we ought to understand that there are any number of people with whom we could have a godly life-long marriage relationship. You see, God doesn't wave a magic wand and bless people with automatically good marriages; they are the product of hard work – mainly in the areas of communication and vulnerability.

I think God gives us the choice about what partner we want to marry, but that doesn't mean we should sit back and wait for the first one to drop into our lap. It's vital that we think about what qualities we're looking for in a partner. Some things will be non-negotiables, while others will have a little flexibility within them. Perhaps one of the most important entries on the list for Christians is the faith of the potential mate. I'm nailing my colours to the mast here and saying that, in my opinion, it's essential when thinking about a marriage partner to look for someone who shares the same faith. If it means everything to you, it's got to mean everything to them too. This has been hotly debated for years, and for every person like me advocating this more conservative position there are ten pieces of anecdotal evidence of gloriously swirling romances where dating evangelism works or true love conquers the divide of religious belief. Fair enough, but for every one of those stories there are a hundred of sadness and slow-burning disillusionment, where both end up without a faith and long-term prospects never seem so good. By making those choices we back away from the best life that God would have us live: full on and at one with him.

As well as someone with the same faith as me, I pray for someone with a 'strong sense of vocation'. The last thing I want to do is get hooked up with someone who doesn't sense that God has a purpose for their life. You might not feel the same about vocation, but if you've got a passion that tugs at your heart strings, it makes sense to me that a potential future partner should feel similarly. There are a few other qualities in the Matt Bird partner prayer, but you'll have to guess the rest 'cause that's all I'm saying.

One of the traps that people who are single often fall into within the Church is to compare themselves to people who are married. As more and more friends marry off, the worry can take up residence in the mind of the ageing single that they might just be the one who is going to be left on the shelf. That's never a nice thought, and I reckon that it's important to keep up with other single people in order to avoid feeling as though you are rapidly becoming a social oddity.

A couple of years ago I was reading about Israel's desire for a king in 1 Samuel. Forgive me for taking it totally out of context, but it really hit me: the Israelites were whinging to God about wanting a king just so that they could be like all the other nations. They were nagging him good and proper, until eventually God said, 'OK, if you want one and won't shut up about it I'll give you a king. But it's not what I want for you and it's not my ideal for you.' This came at a time when I was doing a bit of nagging of God, comparing myself to married couples and wishing that I was part of their club. It seemed as though God might be saying the same thing to me; if I kept it up he'd give me a wife but it wouldn't be his ideal for me at that time. In a sense that was very liberating – knowing that God had things in control – but it also pulled me up sharp; this was serious business, and I didn't want to get into anything that I might regret simply because I was feeling like a snog.

All of this leads us on to the question of just how singles should relate to marrieds. Hopefully we've established that it should not be a two-tier relationship, with marrieds being top dog and singles taking on the role of scum of the earth. However, it can't be denied that sometimes married people can feel uncomfortable inviting a single person round. That often leaves single people feeling like they aren't social currency. I find that frustrating, but it's a challenge that faces both groups, the responsibility to work things out resting on both shoulders.

Being pure in a randy society just isn't easy. Let's face it, wherever we look there seems to be an encouragement to bite into the cherry and have fun. Even in this book we cover sex in chapters on friends and later on shopping, and I think it's fair to say that we do live in the middle of a sex-obsessed society. It seems that with every passing year or two I find Bond films ever more sexist and repugnant. Take that last one, *The World Is Not Enough*; 007's randier-than-thou attitude just didn't do it for me at all, and I found myself cringing. I wasn't alone, and in general the critics gave it a good kicking, deriding it as being out-dated, out of touch and out of time. But one thing it did do was highlight just how much we are surrounded by the crutch-driven urges of media moguls, movers and shakers.

It's hard to live with a pure mind and a clean heart. Jesus had a little to say about it: 'You have heard that it was said, "Do not commit adultery." But I tell you that anyone who looks at a woman lustfully has already committed adultery with her in his heart' (Matthew 5:27–8).

I don't think Jesus said this to discourage every man (or woman) who's ever lived. After all, looking lustfully isn't exactly uncommon round these parts. Instead, I think he mentioned it that we might strive for purity. What's more, Jesus makes it clear that sex isn't merely about what we do physically – you know, with our hands and all that – but it's what goes on in our minds that needs just as much attention.

I used to be an avid reader of *FHM* (*For Him Magazine*), enjoying the playful banter and irreverent slant on life. Then it adopted its 'chicks in bikinis' cover policy. The inside pages weren't much better and I found myself bombarded with all sorts of words and pictures that could be summed up in just one word: unhelpful. So I stopped and moved on to something more refined. My choice was *GQ* (*Gentleman's Quarterly*), an altogether more stylish and adult read. Or at least it was until James Brown, founding editor of *Loaded*, took over. There we were, back with the bikini-clad nymphettes, and again I jacked it in. Now, so long as they stay away from the nude pearl divers of Papua New

Guinea, I feel I'm on safe ground with *National Geographic*.

The truth is that there's so much stuff out there which is not helpful: the sort of stuff that doesn't help develop a pure thought life. It might be terribly repressed and uncool, but I seriously think that we need to put ourselves in a place of total freedom and walk away from it. Other guys, not just me, have done it with *FHM* and *GQ*, and girls have done it with *Cosmopolitan*. There is plenty of stuff out there which isn't helpful for our purity: from places to films, people to art. There's no shame in removing the temptation, in removing things from our sight that cause us to sin. Let's free ourselves from it.

I also think – and this has helped me loads – that we need to be personally accountable to others. This isn't about flogging ourselves in public or giving others a good laugh, but simply drawing strength from the support of our friends. The other members of my prayer triplet and I are each open and vulnerable with the others. We give permission to each other to ask the tough questions and check up things. It helps knowing that people are cheering you on, but also that they understand exactly what things are like for you. Perhaps the most important thing that I have found helpful about being accountable to others is the knowledge that they share a commitment to telling the truth. I'm not going to be left high and dry after a personal revelation; they will share too. That way we don't deal in power, we don't play master and servant. Instead we're all struggling together, helping each other along.

So being single is not awful; far from it. I also have to admit that having been in pastoral situations where I've seen things close up, being in a failing marriage certainly takes the biscuit as far as bum deals go. I can understand why God makes such a big deal about the importance of marriage and hates divorce – not because he wants to heap guilt on divorced people, but simply that he knows how divorce wrecks the lives of everyone involved.

But what about those married people, what about their relationships; what are the pitfalls and peaks? Writing as a single chap you'll have to bear with me, but the following comes out of much talking, thinking and reading, and on a few road tests it seems to have held the bends reasonably well.

First and foremost, all good marriages must be built on the same foundation. I'd even go so far as to say that without this particular discipline present in abundance, the marriage will never really make it out of the shallows. This is as close as you're going to get to a secret formula, so read well: communication. That's it, nothing more mysterious or magical than that: plain old communication.

Before we get on to the 'how', let's look at the 'why'. Communication is to marriage what blood is to bodies, what fuel is to cars. Without it they wither, splutter, wind down and pack up. Why? Because marriage is about two people living together, two – as the Spice Girls sang – becoming one. It kind of makes sense, then, that if these two are going to become one, if they are going to share their lives, be around each other 24/7, make decisions and go through good and bad times together, it makes sense that they know how their partner feels. In any good team the players will be working to a plan, sticking to a strategy, but that doesn't mean that they stop communicating with each other as soon as they make it out on to the pitch. All that dressing-room stuff has been the warm-up – just like going out and getting engaged. It's only once the whistle's been blown that things take off for real. Taking this sports analogy a little further, marriages also fail to run to a script; things happen and circumstances change (whether that be an unexpected bill or a death in the family, trouble at work or plans to start a family), exerting a pressure on the individuals. Because they are just that – individuals – reactions between the two will vary. Hey presto, you've got different things going on in each of the partners. What do you need? Communication. Simple.

So I'm sure that you get the point, but just how do we do it? Some would have you believe that men cannot communicate, that they need to disappear into their caves (be they emotional hideouts or physical ones) and switch off from the continually chatting women. Do yourself a favour, don't believe them. These stereotypes do nothing for relationships and only cause harm. To say that men cannot communicate is to make a claim as ridiculous as saying that women cannot think logically.

We communicate with partners by a simple process; it's called time. That means making time to talk and allowing the habit of good communication to be formed over time. Too many people believe that we should be able to communicate instantly, but it takes both practice and effort. Find a place that works for you; it might be at home sat on the sofa or in bed before you go to sleep. I know of a couple who have a bath together – it's their time to talk, to find out what's really on the other person's mind. You might find it easier to chat while you're walking or out at the pub. Whatever it takes, try experimenting until you find the way that suits both of you best.

Of course, there's plenty more to say about communication, and plenty more has been said far better than I have here, but it's worth a mention, however brief, as it really is the key player. It's not the only big daddy on the block, and the need for compromise rates pretty highly too. Remember that bit in the Bible about 'husbands love your wives and wives submit to your husbands'? I don't think that's a cue for blokes to start playing the fascist dictator around the home any more than it is the woman's cue to abdicate all responsibility for decision-making to the man. Do you really think that the writer meant that the husband was to focus on love but not worry about submission, or that the wife was supposed merely to submit without trying to love? The two are as intertwined as man and woman themselves, and I'm sure that you cannot have true love without being prepared to submit, just as you cannot submit without truly loving. It's not about gender roles or who makes the decisions, it's about being ready to compromise, to love and not count the cost, to prefer the other and not build up resentment. Compromise, just as it is important to friendship, is vital to marriage, if only to make sure that both partners are taking full responsibility for making the relationship work.

## *Life action*

1 If you are a single person and would like a life-long partner, take time out to consider the qualities you are looking for in such a person, and pray to God for a person just like that. Then throw yourself into life and act as if you were going to be single for ever.

2 If you are a single person, consider where you might have been sitting on the runway of life waiting for the plane to take off. Decide to fly now. Ask God to help you feel more like the fully loved and valued child you are.

3 If you're married, consider how your partner is special, unique and perhaps different from you. Go out and buy a card for them and write it to them, telling them how much you appreciate them for who they are.

4 Whether you are married or single you will struggle with sexual temptation. Consider where you struggle; tell one of your closest friends and ask them to pray for you and check on you in that area. They may even reciprocate – if they haven't got someone they are accountable to in that way you'll be doing them a huge favour.

# 5
# *Money and Shopping*

**The scene**
It's undoubtedly one of the greatest socio-economic influences of the day, whether you're talking out-of-town malls and the dramatic effect they've had on the traditional high street, supermarkets and their influence on farming, or ease of credit and equal ease of becoming snared in debt. At the same time we've seen the decline of the Church within the UK, and I wouldn't be the most original person to point out the links between the two.

We've seen the rise in retail therapy – that most delightful of pursuits which cheers us up with a quick pounding of our credit cards. Never underestimate the power of the consumer good to cheer us up – although the chances are that the buzz from the purchase will have long since faded when the monthly statement reminds us of the consequences some time later. Before I start coming off all smug,

I must admit to falling for this one a bit myself; a bad week or stressful day can quite often be just the fuel I need to steer me towards the loving arms of the cash desk. Escape from reality? Not for long.

Then there's leisure shopping, the ideal day out for all the family. Take a trip to your nearest Meadowhall or Bluewater and you can happily while away the hours browsing, buying and trying desperately to keep the kids from peeing in the ornamental fountain.

Fresh on to the scene is Internet shopping – a market that the smart chaps in suits are desperate to corner. The downside for e-stores is that, unlike physical ones, it's dead easy for us to walk out if we don't like the price – after all, the real bargain may be just a couple of clicks away. But it's a double-sided coin, and if it's easy to leave it's even easier to buy; the faceless anonymity of the one-click transaction does away with the final hurdle facing the impulse buyer, that all-important walk up to the cash desk. Many's the time when I've walked out of Dixon's empty-handed thanks to a last-minute stab of common sense prior to making my way up to pay. So how will the on-line shopping experience influence our spending habits? Of course, this is just what e-stores are banking on – the fact that Internet shopping is the way of the future. Proof – if proof were needed – came in 1999 when Tesco laid off almost 20,000 store workers at the same time as announcing a huge financial investment into their dotcom side of things.

Shopping credit seems to be equally available, with almost every retailer ready to hand out their own store card on the spot where you can buy now and pay later at the commendable interest rate of 28.9 per cent APR. Mmmm, tempting, but I think I'll pass. Not sure if it's true, but I heard a story about an eight-year-old who filled out an application form for a credit card that he found in his parents' Sunday paper. The lucky lad got accepted and received a card in the post, although unfortunately his fun stopped there as Mum and Dad intercepted the plastic at the letter box before he had time to pop out to Toys 'Я' Us.

Shopping hyperchoice adds yet another dimension to the activity. Whether it's baked beans or mobiles, we're confronted by choices to be made relating to tariff, salt content, handset, bean juice, network or fat levels, accessories or tiny pork sausages. It's a million miles away from the McDonald's style of things: minimal choice making for rapid decisions, and only occasionally fast service. In many stores it's not uncommon to see people staring blankly at the choice in front of them, easy prey for the commission-hungry salesperson.

We've probably all fallen for the dysfunctional purchase in our time. You'll know if you have because they'll be at the bottom of your wardrobe. Mine include an electric fondue, a jet-wash car cleaner and six dozen pairs of disposable rubber gloves, the sort they wear in *ER* (don't ask). These spontaneous purchases highlight perfectly the tightrope we walk; one slip and we can all too easily end up watery-eyed and skewered by our own shortsightedness (actually, it doesn't show that at all but I'll just leave it there for now).

But hang on a minute, is it all really our fault? Aren't we really the victims? One national newspaper thought so:

'Most of us know the feeling, you get home from the shops, look at what you've bought and think "why on earth did I buy that?" The reason could lie in the range of increasingly sophisticated techniques used by stores to influence what customers buy without them even noticing.'

What sort of techniques? There's zoning – the grouping together of goods in 'must have' sets (like the fleece with the jeans, the accessories with the phones, the select wines with the wine glasses) – and traffic zoning – placing these collections in areas of high traffic like near cash desks, lifts and escalators. Then there's traffic generation, where to encourage people to move throughout the whole of the store they place the essentials – the cash desks, toilets, changing rooms – in the far corners. Hot spots are those strategic sales points, one of the best being the space immediately facing the entrance to the store. There's the music, the lighting, the aroma, temperature and colour, all selected to manipulate the customer's mood. Selling is a science, and guess who are the lab rats?

Our post-modern outlook on life has no respect for yesterday, no hope for tomorrow. It opts to exist in the perpetual present, in the immediate now. What better way to express that present time continuum than in consumerism, the art of the five-second appetite suppressant?

## The value of money
Our response? Well, pull up a seat, pipe and slippers, as there's plenty to say. Far from being a topic that Christians should shy away from, shopping has been part of the Christian manifesto for years. Of course, that's not to say

that a vote for Jesus is a vote for Prada, sweetie. The simple truth is that we do have something to say on the subject. Take Paul, for instance. He wrote that 'the love of money is a root of all kinds of evil'. Sums it up pretty good, no?

I can remember hearing the Argentinean evangelist Luis Palau address the subject by claiming that there's nothing wrong with money. In and of itself, if it's been worked for and earned, there's nothing to condemn it for. But – and this is a sizeable but – the love, desire and hunger for cash can so easily corrupt.

Take Las Vegas, for example, a city in the desert that happens to have one of the ten busiest airports in the world. Of course, the city was founded on money, and the desire to make, win or blag as much cash as possible has sunk deep into the fabric of society there and spawned many further corruptions and illegalities.

When God created the world he took a look and claimed that he'd done a decent job ('it is good' were, I believe, his more exact words). So the material and aesthetic side of things can be enjoyed. Yet we can't deny that certain aspects of it have since been corrupted and spoilt. While we may be able to enjoy a stunning view, an intricate work of art or a fine meal, we are reminded of the fact that we live in a world where some have used their position of power to dominate and oppress others. It kind of leaves a bad taste in your mouth and, like money, the abuse of the good things that God has created can be the cause of all manner of bad things.

How does money motivate us? A simple question this, but an immensely important one. I can remember visiting my bank manager and being asked what my financial ambitions were. I looked blank and he explained that he was interested to know where I saw myself in the wallet department five years hence. I'd understood, but I still looked blank and I struggled to explain that I didn't really have much in the way of financial ambitions. He was surprised – and probably a little disappointed – and over the years it's been a question that I've come back to. Interestingly, a tension has arisen as I've got older; now I do have financial ambitions (keep paying the mortgage, put a little cash aside to live life to the full and have fun) and I can't claim to be the pure white ambition-free financial virgin that I was sitting in the manager's office.

Let's not chuck the baby out with the bathwater, though. Having plans and having responsibilities need not necessarily lump us in with the craving capitalist dogs who work in the city (joke). The key remains this simple question: how does money motivate us? Are we doing everything we can solely in pursuit of a larger wad? What's more, do we take our morals with us into our finances or do we leave them at the door, hoping that no one will notice as we carry out our secret greed-fests.

Lately, people have got wise to the demand from those who want to apply their ethics to their financial dealings. Ethical investment funds came on to the market a few years ago and gave people the chance of investing in companies which exploited neither their workers nor the environment. They were called Brazil funds, as the gag went that you had to be nuts to go for one, but the suppliers were wrong; the funds did well and the consumers proved that their money was not considered separate from their morality.

This idea of there being a right and a wrong way to earn money spills over into our jobs. We can all ask ourselves whether our 9-to-5 is compatible with our beliefs. If it is, all well and good, but if not, do we really think that we can have both integrity and a shady work life?

Of course, this sort of chat is bound to put the wind up people, and it's all too easy to get over-excited and start making foolish claims. The fact is that God doesn't prefer us poor, nor does he like us better when we're loaded. There's a biblical truth that the more we have the more will be asked of us, and while this refers to far more than our salary – just look at the story of the rich young ruler – I'm convinced that this holds the key to a healthy attitude towards money.

Unfortunately for those of us who like the ABC-style prescriptive guide to life, Christianity is fairly oblique on the matter of financial models. Take Acts 2:45 – a ringing endorsement of the socialist model with the New Testament church living as a community: 'Selling their possessions and goods, they gave to anyone as they had need.' Flick back just a few pages and you can find Jesus using a decidedly capitalist example of how money should be used. The Parable of the Talents gives a large thumbs up to wise financial investment and risk-taking.

But instead of getting bogged down with these peripheral concepts, there is common ground which is simply not up for debate. Take poverty, for example. There is absolutely no doubt that Jesus had a special concern for the poor, and Luke goes to greater lengths than any of the other Gospel writers to make this clear. Throughout the book we see Jesus spending time with the lepers and widows, as well as all the other marginalised groups – the tax collectors, Gentiles, women and sick.

God also has an interest in our doing well. This doesn't mean signing up for that old chestnut called the Prosperity Gospel (where God's blessing comes in the form of crisp tenners and highly polished 4x4s), but realising that God can – and often does – help us do well in life. Theologians have spotted a phenomenon that they have called Redemption and Lift. It states that when a person becomes a Christian they often experience social lift. The new integrity, honesty and focus that have been encouraged within them are natural complements to doing well, traits that go down well with any market or employer.

Unfortunately, we can often be quite fond of pointing the finger and declaring others materialistic. We may drive a Ford and be in the clear, but the person in a Merc goes into our books under the column marked Materialist. Because it's all about attitude, God doesn't say that one brand is one side of the line while another brand is in the clear. We're not dealing in absolutes here. Instead, it's all relative. While that might allow the Merc driver a sigh of relief, it also works the other way; Mr Ford could just as likely be guilty of holding on to his Fiesta a little too tightly (a sure guide to materialism).

## Financial ethics

The challenge facing each of us is answering the simple question: have we thought through our financial ethics?

Have we got to grips with the way we earn and spend money? I believe that the foundational principle in this is what King David expressed at the consecration of the temple. 'But who am I and who are my people that we should be able to give as generously as this? Everything comes from you, and we have given you only what comes from your hand.'

So there we go: everything comes from God. Our cars, homes, clothes, savings, families and everything else are all stamped with the God origin logo. By that token everything that we give to God is his already; we're not doing him a huge favour, helping him out while he's a little strapped for cash. Developing this idea then leads us on to question how it informs and directs our attitude towards spending and earning. After all, when we waste money on those dysfunctional purchases, whose money is it that we're wasting? When we hoard treasures, can we really believe that we're storing them up for ourselves?

Shane, a friend of mine who is an independent financial advisor, reckons that you can tell more about a person from their bank statement than anything else. Down there in black and white is a clear depiction of our character, as the things we believe in and the way of life that we value is underlined by our spending patterns. Spotting regular giving on a statement gives my friend an indication of the sort of person he's sitting down with, in much the same way as out-of-control overdrafts and erratic spending binges. But before you go off and check to see that your tithing levels are accurate, it's worth pondering the fact that giving a portion of our income away doesn't immunise us from what we do with the rest. It's all God's – not just 10 per cent of it – and perhaps we ought to spend more time asking him how he wants us to spend his money rather than telling him how we're going to be spending ours. Financial giving is a sign of discipleship, and tithing is a recognition that God has given us everything we need to get by, not a ticket to selfishness and greed.

Unfortunately it's often our bank accounts that are the last parts of our lives to get changed under the influence of Jesus. We can spout off about how much we love him, do all the right moves in the worship meeting and even pray those tastily eloquent prayers that leave others in awe of just how real a relationship we have with Jesus, but our wallets? Forget it, mate: you may be the Son of God but you're not cutting into my fun. Oh dear.

Malachi 3:8 asks 'Will a man rob God? Yet you rob me. But you ask, "How do we rob you?" In tithes and offerings.' Anyone who says that what we earn and own is ours is in the same boat.

Before the coming of Jesus we see Jews as a fairly religious bunch. The Old Testament talks about tithing, giving the firstfruit, the year of Jubilee and so on. When Jesus came he managed to break God's people out of rote submission to rules and servitude. Instead he offered them a new model, one based on grace and the abundance of God's love, kindness and generosity. So we see how giving in the New Testament becomes something that is extravagant and outrageous – just take a look at 2 Corinthians 8:1–15. Still, I reckon we've managed to crowbar things back into shape of late, returning to the religious modes in preference to Jesus' model. Something to be proud of?

## God's provision

I know from my own life that God provides. I've been in financial pickles before, and God has busted me out big time. I remember when the Inland Revenue changed the rules for the self-employed, making us pay our taxes in advance rather than in arrears. It kind of threw me a little to find that I had a whopping tax bill to pay, and I must admit that my first reaction was not prayer or rejoicing at the incoming move of God. Instead, I panicked and got down to some serious worrying. Eventually I came back round to praying, and a little later on met a couple of people, both of whom (and independently of each other) gave me exactly 50 per cent of the bill each.

Then there was the time when my personal organiser got knackered. I was lost without it as I use it to do all my letters, emails, articles, book editing and diary scheduling, and run paperless meetings, so again I began to panic. Then someone offered me the loan of his superior model, which was excellent. Then I felt that God was telling me to buy one for one of my team members. It sounded stupid, so I did it anyway. Next, the one that was bust came back fixed and lovely from the manufacturer, where it had been repaired under guarantee, and was quickly adopted by my personal assistant. Finally, the kind soul who had lent me his turned round and told me to keep it. We were three personal organisers up and God was most definitely in the house. Money is no hurdle for God: what he's more concerned about is having our hearts in tune with his. Issues like obedience and sacrifice suddenly become far more important than cash availability.

From the start of our lives we need to learn how best to earn, spend and give money. Just because you're on pocket money doesn't mean that you cannot start learning how to give and spend wisely. Similarly, those of us who come to faith later on still have time to change the old patterns and replace them with ones more in line with a gospel-oriented view of money. We can discipline ourselves to be generous when we're living on very little, then as God gives us more our good habits will stand us in good stead.

Too often we fall prey to the lame excuses: telling God that we'll put off tithing until we're really earning a decent wage, or avoiding generosity due to our minimal amount of 'disposable' income. In truth there are always reasons why we shouldn't give, and they vary with our age. At first it may be poverty while later it may be financial insecurity. Of course, there will always be a voice that shouts louder, threatening to drown out the cry of generosity. It's all too easy to fall for this one, but it's important to remember that we don't give money to boost God's coffers – as we've said earlier, God doesn't need our cash; he's more concerned with what the acts of earning, spending and giving have to say about the state of our hearts. We need to give to God as a sign that everything we have is his and that we trust him completely to look after us – in whichever way he sees fit.

## A few tips

So how do we sort it out, then? How do we negotiate the minefield of earning, spending and giving without coming a cropper? When it comes to shopping I find it helpful to make a list before I go of whatever it is that I need to buy. It's all too easy to end up tempted by the beautifully displayed goods on special offer, but I speak from bitter personal experience when I say that the aisle of specials does not always lead to the palace of satisfaction. In addition, I don't shop for leisure as I know I'm hopeless at not snapping up a gadget or self-declared 'bargain'.

Second, I try to be conscious of the way in which advertising might be affecting me. So much of what pads out the media is blatant (and sometimes not quite so blatant) advertising for goods that we're told we 'cannot do without' or are 'worth it'. It's important to remain aware of the ploys to bend our arms: after all, if advertising wasn't successful in that aim, there wouldn't be nearly as much of it around, would there? It might make me a little paranoid, but it sometimes helps me to imagine a horde of be-suited ad execs hiding behind the billboards, waiting to pounce on anyone who gets drawn in by their alluring sirens on the poster.

Most of us tend to live beyond our means, so it can also be helpful to work out a budget for the week or month. Take unavoidable outgoings away from income and live on what's left. If you want to be really keen, divide the remnant into sub-sections for the different areas you're likely to want to spend it on. When it's gone, it's gone, but if you can stick to it you've found yourself a sure-fire way of keeping out of debt.

Try asking for financial advice. There are advisors around who can give plenty of assistance when it comes to working out the best way for you to borrow and save. There are also people around (try your local Citizens' Advice Bureau for starters) who can give you solid, practical advice should you find yourself in debt.

### *Life action*

1  Grab last month's bank statement and have a good look. How much do you earn, give and spend? Where does it go? What does it tell you about your character? What would you like your bank statement to say about your character? Make the changes today: money has a powerful way of changing your mind tomorrow.

2  Take out your wallet or purse and chew over the fact that all the money you have comes from God and never stops belonging to him. Pray and ask God to guide you in how you spend every pound that he entrusts to you.

3  Fancy trying something exciting? Highlight everything which is an essential payment next week/month (bills, food, etc.) and fast from spending everything else on non-essentials. Pray and ask God what he would like you to do with that extra money, whether it be large or small. Then have a blast giving it away!

4  Get honest with a friend: tell them what some of your weaknesses are when it comes to the old shopping thing. Discuss together what you might do to put your retail pursuits and habits well in the control of our God.

# 6
## *Culture and Stuff*

**The scene**
Well, of course it's changing – we all know that – but what's interesting about life at the dawn of a sparkling new millennium is the exact type of change that's taking place. I'm not sure if it's happening faster than it ever has done before, and I'm not even sure if the extent of change within culture makes the present day unique. What I do know for sure, however, is the fact that the combined elements that are moulding contemporary culture make for some pretty interesting potential results. If we're serious about this manifesto for life thing, finding the way that our faith works 'in the world', then knowing something about the way that world is changing is bound to be useful. At least, that's what I hope.

## The six oxen of change

Don't ask me why they're oxen, I just like the sound of it, but whatever you call them, the first way in which contemporary Western culture (and in particular that which surrounds us in the UK) is changing is in the realm of spirituality. We're witnessing a shift from what we might call Institutional Spirituality to the bright new button named Societal Spirituality. For decades we've seen the decline of the Church in the UK, with numbers falling and public opinion turning. There have been pockets which have slightly bucked the trend – namely in charismatic evangelical circles – but in general the small surges of growth have been buried under the mass of statistical evidence that points to something approaching a mass exodus. Yet at the same time as the Church has been going through a bout of downsizing, there has been a remarkable rise in the levels of openness in mainstream society. Instead of fitting the term 'secular', there is now an interest in the otherness of life, an acceptance of matters unexplainable that would have been hard to find forty years ago.

In the UK, popular market research has come up with figures of between 70 and 80 per cent for people who believe in some sort of other, higher being. A couple of generations back and you may have come up with the same type of figure, although most people would have called that other being God. Recent research by Gallup shows 96 per cent of Americans believe in God, 90 per cent pray and 71 per cent believe in an afterlife. These days, despite the fact that fewer people have a more formal, church-directed God-consciousness, more perhaps have come to their own conclusions about what might or might not be on the other side of the grave. Take a wander round any bookshop and you'll see a huge range of books filling up the Alternative Spirituality sections, while the space allocated to this type of book has become ever smaller.

Then there's philosophy, the second area in which things have changed. I'm convinced that we're moving from an era of certainty and progress to uncertainty and scepticism (or from modernism to post-modernism, if you like). If you fancy an example, we'll need to dip our toes in the waters of physics, namely Newtonian and quantum. Now, according to Sir Isaac Newton, the way of the world was defined by rigid concepts of cause and effect, development and progress. That cheeky young pup named quantum physics seeks to explain things through chaos theory, random occurrences and the ability of an object to be 'both/ and' (no, I don't understand that bit either). Quantum has sought to replace Newtonian, which has certainly felt the pinch. What we have now is a time of uncertainty and openness, of 'well, I'm not sure, really' as opposed to 'I'm right – so there, you stupid fool' (or something like that).

The wisdom through which we perceive and interpret life is not where it was, isn't yet where it is going and is going to take some length of time to arrive there.

The third area of change which I think is worth having a look at is, I believe, in retail. We've already looked at it in the Money and Shopping chapter, but let's just say here that there's a shift going on between materialism and consumerism. Take Christmas, for instance. I don't think I'd be doing much more than stating the obvious by saying that virtually the whole of Christmas seems to revolve around retail. Not only are the shops trying to squeeze every last potential for credit out of us, but the whole experience – from the presents to the hospitality – focuses the mind on the purchasing of goods. The pressure of measuring the proximity to the festival by the number of remaining shopping days available, coupled with the need to do well and 'put on' a good Christmas, can make for vastly increased stress levels. Add to that the rapid turnaround as the shops start their post-Christmas sales as soon as possible once the big day is over (and sometimes before it has even begun), and you've got quite a situation on your hands. No wonder everyone's broke in February, busy paying off their credit card bills from the previous couple of months.

And so we see the change; we are moving from ownership towards purchasing, from the materialism that encouraged the acquisition of wealth and goods to consumerism, where most satisfaction is derived from the actual act of purchase and consumption.

Of course, there's technology too; the change which has occurred within this field has been phenomenal. We've taken a giant leap from machine technology to information technology, and I'd only bore you if I listed all the innovations that have joined the market within the last few years. From my schooldays I seem to remember being taught how the industrial revolution transformed family and societal life, as industry moved from the cottage to the factory. Well, that transformation is going to appear as nothing compared to the transformation that the technological revolution is bringing to life.

The explosion in the number of Internet cafés has not gone unnoticed, and there are enough people out there who use the net to make it a billion-pound industry. In fact, so much money is tied up in the net that many developing countries are pouring massive amounts of capital reserves into training and research in order that they might skip their place in the manufacturing queue and become world leaders in the Internet revolution.

But hold on just a moment: before half of us have got our heads around the idea of the Internet, along comes Internet mark II (I2): bigger, badder and with even more knobs on. Here's what *The Economist* had to say about it:

> The I2 network is named Abilene after the railhead that opened America's west. It is based on a new protocol, Ipv6 – you currently use Ipv4 – and currently wires up universities. This new protocol has massive capacity, is super-reliable and much, much faster than today's congested info-highway. Abilene can transfer data at 2.4 gigabits a second, 45,000 times faster than a typical modem; imagine ten encyclopaedias sent around the world in less than a second.
>
> 'The World in 2000'

A recent article entitled 'The end of the vowel' caught my eye in an edition of *The Face* magazine:

> Text messaging is fast becoming one of our key methods of communication. It was only last winter that mobile

phone users became able to text-message other networks, at which point a minor, geeky plaything exploded into a cross-cultural phenomenon. It's cheap, popular (usage increased by 3,000 per cent between spring 1998 and winter 1999) and has been enthusiastically adopted by the all-important youth consumer. No one in the industry predicted this: the popularity of the service has taken them by surprise and, for once, the street has led the manufacturers and marketers. And with the next generation of wireless application protocol (WAP) phones, the main point of Internet access is set to move from computer to phone. The text-messaging trend is also having a radical impact on the way we use language. The most important restriction on the technology is the 160-character limit, which in turn shapes the way we use and abbreviate written English: brevity remains the single most crucial consideration. As text-messaging and emails become our favoured forms of written communication, they will alter the ways in which we use words, grammar and punctuation. Were Primal Scream right? Wll th vwl dsppr?

Quite simply, technology is moving at an incredible speed, becoming ever smaller, ever faster and ever cheaper. The IT revolution will have an even greater impact on family life than the industrial revolution, although quite what things will look like is anyone's guess. After all, as Tim Berners-Lee (the man who invented the Internet) said: 'If we know what the future is, we aren't looking far enough ahead.' Linked to the changes in technology is the fifth main ox of change: communication. We have moved from text-based communication to image-based communication. That's not to say that we'll be packing up and heading back to using hieroglyphics, but that the primary medium of communication is image over text. Try taking out the words from a magazine and the chances are that you'll still be left with a fair amount left over. Perhaps we're moving in favour of the Internet way of doing things: interactive text – cyber text – which enables two-dimensional reading. Bill Gates wrote this in an article entitled 'Beyond Guttenberg' (a reference to the first printing press that enabled the multiple production of books):

> Reading on paper is so much a part of our lives that it's hard to imagine that anything could ever replace inky marks on shredded trees. Since Johannes Guttenberg invented an economical way to make moveable metal type in the fifteenth century, making it possible to produce reading matter quickly, comparatively cheaply and in large quantities, the printed word has proved amazingly resilient. So how could anyone believe that sales of electronic books could exceed those of paper books within a decade or so?

Mr Gates goes on to make his case for such a change. Optimistic he may be, but if he's right the changes could be astounding. We already have the MP3 – enabling the user to download music direct from the Internet on to their pc and on to a portable player – how long before this becomes the way we buy books?

The sixth and final change we're looking at in our culture is in terms of geography. We're experiencing a move from colonial imperialism to global fragmentation. It might sound rather quaint now (or not, depending on your politics), but the British Empire shrank comprehensively throughout the twentieth century. Devolution has left its mark on Scotland and Wales, and Northern Ireland is certainly in a different state than it was in the mid-1990s.

We've seen the growth of our 'Global Village' as the planet seems to get ever smaller, thanks to the influence of technology on areas of communication, commerce and travel. Bizarrely, I'll often get a quicker reply to an email if the recipient is in America than if they happen to be in the UK – the time lag means that they get them first thing in the morning and I usually hear back by the time I'm turning off my pc at the end of the day. In terms of travel, it's cheaper and quicker to fly to Amsterdam, Paris or Dublin (thanks to the low-cost airlines) than it is to travel by train from London to Yorkshire. No wonder it seems as if the world is shrinking, especially when you add into the mix the spread of multi-national concerns like Coca-Cola, McDonald's and so on. Even in Dhaka, Bangladesh, I saw a McDonald's and a Burger King, as well as posters for Geri Halliwell's debut solo album. I wish I could say that it felt comforting to be surrounded by the familiar, but somehow it didn't quite seem so good.

Ironically, while relative to travel and communication the world is getting smaller and increasingly homogenised, it is also fragmenting at the basic levels. Societies and their basic building blocks – the family – are experiencing terrific pressure, and many seem to be going under.

## The stuff that surrounds us

A few years back I visited Estonia – a country I'd never been to before. It was great, but went down as a highly bizarre trip on the basis of just one evening. The rest of the travelling crew and I were having dinner with a local family. They didn't speak much in the way of English and we were pretty sparse on the Estonian front, but they invited us along to their home and we were dead happy to accept. Before we sat down to eat, the man managed – through an elaborate game of charades – to ask us whether we'd like to have a sauna. Naturally we nodded yes, and he beckoned us to follow him towards the back of the house. Us chaps went into the changing room and slowly undressed, checking carefully to make sure that no one was going to go the whole hog and remove their boxers. Our host was not so shy, and whipped off his kecks without any sense of embarrassment. Of course, we knew we had to follow suit, so we did, if a little self-consciously.

It was then time to make our way to the sauna where the coals were burning up a treat. Our host was cranking it up, chucking plenty of water on and making sure we were getting good and hot. After ten minutes or so he sprang up and indicated that we should do the same. We did, and were then encouraged to turn our backs to him and bend over the bench we had been sat upon. To say we were unsure would be to put it mildly. He remained insistent, and it was only because there were five of us that we decided to do as he said. Our worst fears were almost realised when, in between glances up and down the line at each other, we looked down and saw him reach into a bucket and pull out a fistful of beech branches. He proceeded to thwack each one of us soundly from ankle to backside to neck. When we were all done he indicated that we were to turn around and receive more of the same on our fronts. Hands were used strategically, and it remains one of the most 'interesting' cross-cultural experiences I've ever come across.

There's a magazine called *Wallpaper* – a splendidly pretentious magazine at that – which is subtitled 'The Stuff that Surrounds Us'. That's precisely what culture is – the stuff that greets us at every turn. Steve Chalke once defined it as 'the glue that holds society together', and it often takes on the role of intergenerational delivery agent. Tradition and attitude, aspiration and fear, they all get passed down from parent to child, and it's safe to say that culture is also infinitely malleable; just a few people living together will start to form their own microculture, with dress, language and attitudes that mark them apart as a group.

Yet what is it in us that makes us need culture, what is it that makes us need to be part of a group? There has always been a tribal instinct within the human race, a desire to be in it with a group of people who do things the same way. In part it is to do with our instinct for survival.

Sociologists have observed that every twenty years there is a generational shift, a fundamental change in attitudes and practice that marks the difference between generations, each with their own distinctive identities. Right now we're living among a whole host of generations: millennials,

X, boomers, busters and so on. What Graham Cray, an Anglican culture vulture, describes is something called Cultural Shift: the process that occurs every two to three hundred years. This massive paradigm (or model) shift takes place within culture. The last time we went through such a change was at the time of the industrial revolution and, you guessed it, we're riding one right now.

A senior Microsoft engineer recently said that 'it's not about learning curves any more – it's about forgetting curves'. It's not just about taking on new knowledge, but it's about forgetting all that we've learnt before that has been rendered obsolete by the latest upgrade. This is particularly pertinent to technology, but it also comes into play in wider areas: business practice, social policy, art and so on.

Richard Eyre, the former chief executive officer of ITV, picked up on this when he was working for the company. He said that it was: 'A great corporation, a great organisation, that in 1997 had, frankly, a past that was more exciting that its future.'

The question I believe we need to face up to is: how much is this opinion about ITV relevant to us? How much of our past is actually going to be more exciting than our future because we refuse to adapt to the new culture in which we're living?

## Need for flexibility

Companies that find themselves rigid and inflexible will also find themselves collapsing and failing in the new, emerging culture. Companies, on the other hand, that are flexible and responsive to the context in which they find themselves will be set to thrive. It's like being on a plane at 30,000 feet. You look out of the window at the wings, and what are they doing? Bouncing, most likely. There's an inbuilt flexibility that is vital if you're not going to have a couple of snapped wings on your hands. Or there's the Eiffel Tower. If you've been up to the top on a windy day you'll have noticed that it does tend to move somewhat. Instead of this being M. Eiffel's idea of zuh leetle joke, again it's a central component of its success: without flexibility it would snap (probably).

I'm studying for an MBA at the moment – a course that's teaching me loads about business. One of the things that we've found out is the nature of the successful company. It turns out that if you want to have a successful business on your hands you're going to have to get to grips with the idea of product lifecycle and the need to develop it to relate to the ever-changing market. The theory goes that no product has an eternal lifespan. Organisations need to keep a near-constant eye out for the market response, being able to predict in advance the time when your particular brand of foot deodoriser starts to lose market share. Before it's too late the product has a little make-over and is summarily re-launched, ready to start another journey along the curving tracks of consumer demand. Simple as that.

There's a fascinating man named Charles Handy who is something of a management guru. He has written about a lot of things, but one in particular stands out here: the theory of the sigmoid curve. It's a simple 'S' shape – but lying on its side – and it recognises that a product needs a lot of resources and inertia to get off the ground. As its life progresses the amount of resources needed to help promote it will decline and profit will increase. Because Handy doesn't see growth as straight, he believes that eventually growth will taper off, much like the curve at the top of the 'S'. The trick, then, is to get to the product and reinvent it just before profitability and growth start to head downwards. You do that by taking the best of the old and adapting it to the new.

This is precisely the challenge that faces us as individuals: are we prepared to adapt to the culture in which we're living in order that we might remain a relevant and necessary voice? If we're not, the chances are that we'll end up retreating and living in a religious ghetto. There are three positions that you can take in relation to this challenge. First, you can live against culture, taking a fundamentalist position; viewing new culture as sinful and wrong, you'll be caught up with concepts about how the devil and his demons are running wild in 'the world'. Second, you can take the chance to adopt the culture, assuming a liberal position. Here everything is taken on board without any form of critique or analysis being applied. Third, you can opt for the missionary position (my personal favourite), where you mix and match the first two.

## Adopting the good

Parts of culture are good and need to be taken on board so that we might communicate with society. After all, this is the basis of Christianity: God became man incarnate and he chose to place himself in a specific culture, at a specific time. As John 1:14 says, 'The Word became flesh and blood, and moved into the neighbourhood.' God sent a message out loud and clear: culture is not something to be avoided. Therefore Christianity is founded on the basis of God adapting to culture.

There's no doubt that we are living in a cross-cultural context: the landscape around us has changed so much that we now find ourselves living in a different place. We're faced with the challenge of being relevant. Like Sony, we need to be aware of the world around us. In an advert for the Play Station game Cool Boarders, they ran the following copy:

It gets into your system. The music rushes round your head. The adrenaline courses through your body. Stopping is not an option. First you're racing to win, then you're fighting to survive. One moment you're marvelling at how real everything seems, the next you can't believe that sheer depth and scale of what you're getting into. No side effects are yet known but the potential is widespread. With over 300 different ways of getting the bug and one in ten households affected, no one is immune.

By using the language of the drug scene they proved a point: messages can be adapted. Sony had adapted to the language of the drug scene so well that the ad got banned, but you get the point.

Interestingly, this is nothing new, and the Apostle Paul was at it years ago. He said that he was willing to 'become all things to all men' so that he might save some of them by whatever means possible (1 Corinthians 9:22).

## Alien 1

Think about the Old Testament's retelling of the story of Daniel. A Hebrew, he was born among the Israelites and was very much part of the furniture, fitting in with his home culture. Then he got exiled from Jerusalem and wound up in Babylon, where he came face to face with an entirely different culture. Not only did he face a new language and literature, but he had his name changed to one that sounded like one of the Babylonian gods. Third, he was forced to eat rich food and wine. Suddenly life was no longer black and white; he could no longer continue to apply his old set of religious ways of behaviour, and he was facing dilemmas his faith had never prepared him for. The landscape had changed, and he had to remould his religion to mean anything in the new place. He learnt the language and the literature, went along with the name change, but he made an issue over the diet. He ended up going vege-tarian – thinking about it I reckon I'd probably have gone along with learning the language and the literature (although it might have taken me a little longer than Daniel), I wouldn't have been so willing to have my name changed but I certainly wouldn't have had a problem with the fine food and wine. New cultures require us to live in the grey, in the areas where no one has pioneered before, where we have to ask hard questions of our faith and be prepared to strip away tradition from its pure essence.

## Alien 2

Look at Paul in the New Testament. He was a zealous Christian-killer, a top-notch Jew through and through.

Having rather rudely had his life interrupted by Jesus Christ he became a Christian and later travelled to a strange city (Athens) where he met an alien culture. Instead of walking around telling people exactly where they were going wrong, condemning sinners and whipping up a storm, he went on a wander and surveyed the landscape, absorbing the culture. When he stood up to communicate his faith he quoted their poets and sayings. He even held up a picture of the idol credited to a foreign God, finding a way to communicate his faith in a foreign land.

This is our challenge, too. The culture in which we live is radically different from the Christian ghetto some of us have grown up in.

## A few tips

What we need to do now is to learn how to live the Christian life in the missionary position, not ghetto-style. Perhaps I can suggest a few practical things that we can do to help ourselves along.

First up, we need to decide what are the core essentials of the gospel. What are the values of the King and the kingdom that are completely non-negotiable? Try reading through the Gospels and pulling out the values from which you would not deviate. It's all there – compassion, purity, relationship and truth – but you'll be surprised at how much you're left with that has been part of your Christian subconscious that has little basis in the life of Jesus. Write those gospel-inspired non-negotiables down and be clear about what it is that you think are fundamentals. After that, it's time for the difficult stuff: adapting to a mindset that is prepared to reconsider anything else.

Some of the things that we believe are not quite so perfect as we might have previously thought. Here are a few facts about evangelicals from the Gallup Organisation's research in the United States:

| | Born again | Not born again |
|---|---|---|
| Use alcohol | 25% | 75% |
| Smoke cigarettes | 41% | 53% |
| Family drink problem | 40% | 52% |
| Family gambling problem | 36% | 51% |
| Pro-choice when it comes to abortion | 33% | 58% |
| Belief that homosexuality is something one is born with | 29% | 65% |
| Believe in ghosts | 28% | 31% |
| Believe in reincarnation | 20% | 24% |
| Have consulted a fortune teller | 16% | 17% |
| Believe in astrology | 26% | 24% |

This research shows us that perhaps we haven't got some of our beliefs quite right and we are more confused about stuff than we think. Many of the sacred cows we cherish need to be taken out and slaughtered (some of our old non-negotiables need to become negotiable). Some of what we have thrown away we need to go and dig out of the bin quick (some of our negotiables need to become non-negotiables fast).

Third, having worked out what is non-negotiable and what is up for grabs, we need to step out into the culture in which we live and we need to absorb it. We need to lap it up, to look at it, examine it, critique it and adapt to it when we feel that we can use it to communicate the eternal values of the kingdom of God. Those things that are contrary to the gospel we need to hold at a distance. It'll be tough, though; we'll discover that many of the things that we've held dear have actually been surplus to requirements. For the sake of doing our job and spreading the gospel, we need to adapt.

Take the film *Dogma*. It was out at the tail end of 1999 and it caused quite a fuss. I received a copy of an email from a friend of a friend, rather strongly encouraging Christians not to go and see the film. It was, the original petitioner had said, full of bad language, and it ridiculed Christianity. I'd seen it and, yes, the language wasn't so good, but as for ridiculing our faith I wasn't so sure. It made me laugh at myself and my fellow church members, which is surely no bad thing – where in the Bible does it tell us to be mealy-mouthed miseries? Anyway, a huge email debate ensued, with people getting reasonably hot under the collar on both sides of the argument.

Writer/director Kevin Smith attended Our Lady of Perpetual Help Parochial School, where he came across Sister Theresa's unusual perspective in his religion class:

'Jesus was being facetious when He called Peter a rock,' she informed us. 'He knew that Peter was the weakest of the apostles, and He knew, too, that Peter would betray

Him three times during His passion.'

'How'd He know that?' someone foolishly asked.

'Because He was God,' she patiently replied. 'But He was also a man – a human being. And He had a sense of humour. Here was His wishy-washy friend Peter, who He knew was a guy with very little backbone, and couldn't exactly be counted on just yet. And Christ was having a little fun with him, at his expense, telling Peter he was a rock, and winking at the other apostles who also knew that Peter was like a reed in the wind: bending whichever way the wind blew.'

'Wait a second,' I asked (after raising my hand, of course). 'Christ was picking on Peter when He called him a rock?'

'In fun, yes. He was teasing his friend – not unlike the way you tease your friends, Kevin.'

And with that, Sister Theresa did something for me that no one had ever tried to do before, and gave me something that has remained with me ever since.

She humanised Christ.

I consider *Dogma* a psalm of sorts (albeit one with a few dick and fart jokes thrown in). It's my love-letter to God and to faith – which is about the only thing we really truly have in life.

I find it interesting that what one person can see as a heresy, another can view as a love-letter to God. That gives me hope, especially as I'm convinced that the culture we live in is full of opportunities. We're faced with a simple choice, as Patrick Dixon, Director of Global Change, puts it:

'Either we take hold of the future or the future will take hold of us.' Perhaps too is the danger that we'll refuse to let go of the past.

### Life action

1  Over the next few weeks read the Gospels, and as you do so write down the non-negotiable values of the kingdom of God. You might want to write down a value when it appears, then note how many other times it appears as you read through the Gospels. You might well be surprised by what is and what isn't there.

2  Be very honest with yourself: what are some of the things in your faith that you make a big deal of that Jesus didn't fuss over or maybe never even mentioned? Pray and sacrifice these sacred cows.

3  Sit down with a friend and discuss how the culture in which you live has changed even in the last five years. Then make a note of some of the trends and themes that you see in the world you live in.

# 7

# *Justice and Society*

## The scene

You don't have to be a genius to work out that the world is scarred with the presence of injustice. Wherever you look – at home or abroad, through the media or in the lives of friends – there are instances where fairness and 'the right thing' are deliberately ignored, where those who hold the power openly abuse those who don't. The human race has a mandate to sit up, take notice and act whenever we hear of injustice, but its proliferation leads many to believe that we've not been taking the job quite as seriously as we might.

The history books are peppered with examples of oppression and denial. But this history – while both shocking and relevant to us today – can sometimes be too easily ignored. The truth is that the world we are living in today needs sorting out, and while many are taking up the challenge, there is still plenty more that humankind can do to make new history.

Perhaps the greatest of all injustices are the numbers of street children around the world. UNICEF puts their number at 100 million worldwide, a figure which can be divided into roughly three groups. There are the children who are dependent on the street for survival during the day, yet who will sleep at for what passes as a family home at night. This is perhaps the largest group, and while they are on the street they are not only highly vulnerable but are missing out on education and childhood. The second group are the children of the street. They may have some contact with their family, but in general they are denied the assurance of daily family support. They are easy targets for exploitation, and represent the middle ground between the first and the third group: street children themselves. These are the children who have nothing. They are solely reliant on the street for everything they need: shelter, sustenance, protection. Needless to say, they rarely have enough of any of these. If only there were safety in numbers: there are 10 million of these children worldwide, and they can be found in every country.

In London, one of the biggest issues facing those fighting for fairness and equality is the problem of homelessness. Innovative projects like *The Big Issue* have helped address some of the problems facing this large group of people. The definition of the term 'homeless' includes not only rough sleepers but those in shelters and temporary accommodation as well.

But injustice stretches beyond the street. There's the

horrific situation of AIDS being passed from mother to unborn child, from rapist to victim, from the infected to the recipient of blood transfusion, from one lover to another. In the year 2000 it was estimated that worldwide 16,000 people each day contracted AIDS, and in many cases it is not only ignorance that is to blame. In Africa alone, more than 20 million people have been diagnosed as being HIV positive.

The UK has begun to wake up to the extent of the poverty that surrounds us. Previously we buried facts under statistics and figures, claiming that it was part of the class system and something to be either ignored or accepted. Recent research has made clear the links between poverty and poor education, health and other social problems. While using poverty as an excuse can be risky, it's important to own up to at least a two-tier society and begin to question the self-serving nature of middle England, a system which I believe would rather things remained just as they are, thank you very much.

The late Bernie Grant, MP for Tottenham – one of the poorest boroughs in Greater London – enquired of Camelot about the amount of money spent by his constituents on the National Lottery and the amount of direct funding awarded as grants to projects working within his constituency. The shocking results were that between 1994 and 2000 his constituency spent £63 million on the Lottery (the national average per constituency being only £38 million). In return they received only £5 million back in grants. It is a shocking injustice that company directors line their pockets with the profits made from cynical manipulation of people's aspirations. Time and again we hear of people caught in the 'if only' trap, believing, as they are told, that life would be better if only the jackpot was theirs, yet increasing their financial burden by taking part.

Racism has been something of a hot potato recently. At the time of writing there's an apparent political belief that playing the nationalist card on the issue of asylum seekers is a real vote-winner. It's widely accepted that as the levels of such talk increase, so too do the number of racist attacks. In a recent by-election, William Hague was accused by the far-right British National Party of 'nicking our policies' on immigration, while at the same time the government has repeatedly gone back on an earlier pledge not to use inflammatory language like 'bogus' and 'flood' when discussing those seeking asylum in the UK.

All of this comes hot on the heels of the Macpherson Inquiry into the police handling of the murder of Stephen Lawrence. The then chief commissioner of the Metropolitan Police admitted that there was institutional racism within the police force. The final report described it like this:

> The collective failure of an organisation to provide an appropriate and professional service to people because of their colour, culture or ethnic origin. It can be seen or detected in processes, attitudes and behaviour which amount to discrimination through unwitting prejudice, ignorance, thoughtlessness and racist stereotyping which disadvantage minority ethnic people.

It's frightening to think that an organisation which is one of the guardians of the founding principles of our society is guilty as charged. But it goes further than that, and as culture shifts we are all faced with the challenge of examining ourselves for the legacies of racism that may remain from a time where inclusivity and acceptance were not so highly prized.

I was inspired by a letter of response that Martin Luther King made to a group of religious leaders:

> So often the contemporary church is a weak, ineffectual voice with an uncertain sound. So often it is an arch defender of the status quo. Far from being disturbed by the presence of the church the power structure of the average community is consoled by the church's silence, and often even vocal sanction of things as they are. If the judgement of God is on the church like never before, if today's church does not recapture the sacrificial spirit of the early church it will lose its authenticity, forfeit the loyalty of millions and be dismissed as an irrelevant social club with no meaning for the twentieth century. Every day I meet young people whose disappointment with the church has turned into outright disgust.

The spectre of racism remains more than just a blip on the viewscreen; the Church still faces the same challenge.

Yet that's not to say that Christians haven't gone to the wall for their beliefs of late. I'm not sure just how polite it is to use them as a measure of 'success', but there were more Christian martyrs during the last century than in any previous. I was moved when I visited Westminster Abbey recently and saw the statues representing ten of those martyrs. As I read the short biographies on each martyr, one about an African girl struck me in particular:

Father Augustine Moaca established a mission at Maurican where the chief was happy to see missionaries from all faiths live and work. It was with her cousin Kia that Manche Masemola first heard Moaca preach. She wanted to hear more and began to attend classes twice a week. Fearful that she would leave them or refuse to marry, her parents sought to discourage her but she defied them. She was beaten and on a number of occasions Manche Masemola remarked to Moaca that she would die at their hands. Then on or near the 4th February 1928 her mother and father took her to a lonely place and killed her at the age of 15 years old.

The lack of religious freedom in many countries today is a crime. Ironically, it was only a few years later that Manche's mother became a Christian, was baptised and returned to the grave of the daughter she had killed.

I have a friend who moved from America to work among his own people in a developing country, as leader of a relief organisation there. He and his wife decided to have a child, but when the baby boy was just a few days old tragedy struck as the doctor at the local hospital administered the wrong medicine. It was a horrific mistake, yet the lack of resources, training and funding all go to make standards of healthcare around the globe both unequal and unfair. If these friends had chosen to stay in their comfort zone they would have a son today.

The environment has received plenty of attention in recent decades, yet while most of us are aware of the dangers the damage is still clearly being done. Industrial and domestic pollution continue to wreak havoc, yet the implications of changing over to more environmentally sound practices have significant financial implications for governments and multi-nationals. Of course, nothing changes, and each week we continue to burn fossil fuels despite the fact that the average British home has the potential to meet 100 per cent of its energy requirements from renewable sources. It's crazy but true; local opposition to wind farms (those majestic-looking white columns with what looks like a propeller on the top) has been immense in the UK, even though they represent significant potential to avert the fast-looming energy crisis.

## What's justice all about?

First they came for the Communists, but I was not a Communist – so I said nothing.

Then they came for the Social Democrats, but I was not a Social Democrat – so I did nothing.

Then came the trade unionists, but I was not a trade unionist.

And then they came for the Jews, but I was not a Jew – so I did little.

Then when they came for me, there was no one left who could stand up for me.

Martin Niemöller (1892–1989)

At the end of the day, pursuing justice is about being in a right relationship with the whole of creation. It's about saying that you're not willing to accept the fact that men and women are sleeping rough on the streets near your home. It's about saying that you're not willing to accept institutional racism at the heart of a major public service. It's about being unwilling to accept the misuse of the environment or the inequalities between health resources in different countries.

Look at a dictionary definition of justice and you'll see stuff about fairness, but also about 'the exercise of authority in the maintenance of right'. You see, justice is an active concept, one that involves bringing resolution to conflict. Justice cannot be justice if something doesn't happen to assist in the exercise of authority in maintenance of right. And, of course, this is where we come at it: God is the authority maintaining right, and we assist in that process. Like Niemöller himself, if we remain paralysed by fear or indecision, if we fail to act, then we cannot really claim to be pursuing justice.

## Living with bad stuff

But, of course, all the stuff at the start of this chapter underlines the message that we're living in a world where justice isn't always winning through. That doesn't mean that God isn't in charge, that his authority is somehow too frail to cope. I tend to think that it has more to do with our – as a human race – choosing selfishness and greed over fairness and justice. The Bible draws on this right at the start. Read from Genesis 1 onwards and you'll get the stories of creation and rebellion, followed by this: 'The LORD saw how great man's wickedness on the earth had become, and that every inclination of the thoughts of his heart was only evil all the time' (Genesis 6:5).

The basic or default condition of our society is one of corruption. Fertile ground for injustice, the human can easily become distracted from God's own Eden and focus on very human appetites.

Paul expands on this when he writes about the replacing of the old order of things with the new one:

I consider that our present sufferings are not worth comparing with the glory that will be revealed in us. The creation waits in eager expectation for the sons of God to be revealed. For the creation was subjected to frustration, not by its own choice, but by the will of the one who subjected it, in hope that the creation itself will be liberated from its bondage to decay and brought into the glorious freedom of the children of God.

We know that the whole creation has been groaning as in the pains of childbirth right up to the present time. Not only so, but we ourselves, who have the firstfruits of the Spirit, groan inwardly as we wait eagerly for our adoption as sons, the redemption of our bodies. For in this hope we were saved. But hope that is seen is no hope at all. Who hopes for what he already has? But if we hope for what we do not yet have, we wait for it patiently.

In the same way, the Spirit helps us in our weakness. We do not know what we ought to pray for, but the

Spirit himself intercedes for us with groans that words cannot express.

Romans 8:18–26

Like Paul, we are living with the tension of knowing the way of society now, at the same time as knowing something of the way it will be in the future. This is a difficult situation to be in and can bring up all sorts of questions, from 'Why the delay, huh, God?' to 'What role does prayer take in the advancement of the kingdom?' But there's one topic linked to this that never fails to confuse and ignite. I call it the Theology of Bad Stuff, and it centres on this simple question: 'Where is this almighty, loving and powerful God when bad stuff happens?'

Unfortunately there are no quick answers, no watertight solutions to the presence of bad stuff in a God-ordained universe. Sorry about that, but it's the truth. However, there are things that need to be said, truths which need to be pointed out so that we might have a wider perspective. Very often we have to live with the knowledge that we are caught in the middle of transforming into the perfect, a time that is on its way towards becoming the way God intended. The presence of injustice reminds us of just how far away we can be from the presence of God's kingdom, but instead of being a cause for misery this can stir us on to fight injustice and bring more of God's flavour into the world.

But there's more to it than that: acting for justice is not an optional extra – it is our responsibility. God has asked us to take responsibility for creation: 'God blessed them and said to them, "Be fruitful and increase in number; fill the earth and subdue it. Rule over the fish of the sea and the birds of the air and over every living creature that moves on the ground" ' (Genesis 1:28).

Even later, when we read the story of Cain and Abel, we get to the point where God asks Cain where his brother is. 'Am I my brother's keeper?' comes Cain's reply. The implication is clear: we have a responsibility to those who live around us. We are not isolated individuals free from obligation to others. We are accountable, and there's no getting out of it.

## An alternative society

In thinking about justice and society we've touched on this idea of God having other plans for the way things should be. The Bible is full of references to this, with talk of the new heaven and the new earth, the kingdom being at hand and a time when the old will pass away and the new will take over. There's plenty of this in Revelation, where the idea gets fleshed out a little, as we read about a time when there are no more tears and there is no more pain.

Of course, that all sounds very nice, but what does it have to do with us, right here, right now? Are we supposed to be trying to recreate temporary Virtual Heavens, to get out the angel costumes and brush up on our celestial harp skills? Methinks not. The truth is that the picture of heaven is as gutsy as it comes, and building it in the earthly present is a million miles away from the spiritual platitudes and vagaries that some seem to favour. The point about there being no more tears in heaven should not lead us to believe that there will be no more tear-ducts – it's not that we'll be ditching our fragile physicality in favour of rugged 'spiritness'. It means that God's dynamic rule will be such that sadness – and the injustice which so often causes it – will have no place at all. That means that we are recreating earth so that we know heaven in the here and now on earth. That's good news for us Christians, and it's a decent kick up the butt for us to carry on marching forward in the name of justice, further on from the old order of things and into something new (although not exclusive to our generation) and exciting.

The Old Testament talks a lot about what this type of new society may look like. While we might usually turn to it only to fuel up for some heated debate about homo-sexuality or handy hints on how to deal with troublesome mildew, we might be surprised by some of the more, shall we say, practical content. Try this on for size:

> When you reap the harvest of your land, do not reap to the very edges of your field or gather the gleanings of your harvest. Do not go over your vineyard a second time or pick up the grapes that have fallen. Leave them for the poor and the alien. I am the LORD your God.
>
> Do not steal.
>
> Do not lie.
>
> Do not deceive one another.
>
> Do not swear falsely by my name and so profane the name of your God. I am the LORD.
>
> Do not defraud your neighbour or rob him.

Do not hold back the wages of a hired man overnight.

Do not curse the deaf or put a stumbling-block in front of the blind, but fear your God. I am the LORD.

Do not pervert justice; do not show partiality to the poor or favouritism to the great, but judge your neighbour fairly.

Do not go about spreading slander among your people.

Do not do anything that endangers your neighbour's life. I am the LORD.

Do not hate your brother in your heart. Rebuke your neighbour frankly so that you will not share in his guilt.

Do not seek revenge or bear a grudge against one of your people, but love your neighbour as yourself. I am the LORD.

Leviticus 19:9–17

OK, so some of the suggestions about farming technique and keeping money overnight might not be so relevant to the shopworker from Ipswich, but that's missing the point. Look at the heart of what is being said, and it's clear that justice is being screamed out loud and clear. It's also clear that justice can be promoted by small, practical measures – giving food, offering spare resources free of charge to those without, paying promptly and fairly – a fact which, in our attempt to appear holy, we too often overlook.

That's not to say that big plans don't have their place either. Later the book mentions something called the 'year of Jubilee'. The plan was that every forty-nine years land would be returned to owners, debts would be wiped out, and so on. A wonderful idea, yet it never quite happened. I wonder why?

The New Testament offers the wonderful story of the Good Samaritan. It's so common that we forget just how much of a deal it was for the Samaritan to help the Jew – such was the enmity between their two people. Surely his behaviour was a perfect model of justice, of new relationships overcoming old prejudices?

Sadly, we have so often slipped into meaningless debate about what actually constitutes justice. We split things up into evangelism and social action, claiming that things are best done when they lead to some form of repentance and belief. Many see acts of justice as second best, as less important relatives of the real deeds of the kingdom. This has its roots in something called the Great Reversal, a period in the nineteenth century where the Church split into various and often opposing factions. Today we are left in awkward situations, often at risk of failing to grasp the full breadth of the Christian message. If we favour one strand over the other, we're bound to miss out.

I'm convinced that, from God's perspective, evangelism and social action are completely indivisible. In the life and the work of his Son, Jesus, we read about his manifesto for life. It was packed with words, works and wonders, and kicked off with him declaring his revolutionary intent: 'The Spirit of the Lord is on me because he has anointed me to preach good news to the poor. He has sent me to proclaim freedom for the prisoners and recovery of sight for the blind, to release the oppressed, to proclaim the year of the Lord's favour' (Luke 4:18–19).

These words are pure revolution, pure upside-down-turning logic. Nothing could be the same again, yet still we have people who come along today and take various elements away from it. Removing the actions, some claim that Jesus' manifesto was based on words and preaching. Taking away the words and preaching, others claim that he came to get on with the works and action. Others still underemphasise the words and works and claim that it's all about the miracles and the power of the Holy Spirit. In reality Jesus never made those distinctions. Instead he had a holistic view, one which happily integrated all elements. Interestingly, Jesus' execution was a political one, designed to appease those who saw him as a threat to the status quo.

Douglas Coupland's book *Girlfriend in a Coma* tells the stories of a few people, one of whom – you guessed it – slips into a coma. Things get a little apocalyptic towards the end and the narrator gives the characters the opportunity to stand back and face the following challenge:

In your old lives you had nothing to live for, now you do. You have nothing to lose and everything to gain. Go clear the land for a new culture, bring your axes, scythes and guns. I know you have the necessary skills; explosives, medicine, engineering, media knowledge and the ability to camouflage yourselves. If you're not spending every moment of your waking lives radically rethinking the nature of the world, if you're not plotting every moment, boiling the carcass of the old order, then you're wasting your day.

I believe that sort of philosophy is at the heart of our manifesto. We ought to be people working for revolution, working hard to usher in an alternative society, one founded on the values and principles of the kingdom of heaven. So often Christianity is reduced to something that we term 'spiritual' but that in reality is utterly spineless, made up of preaches about fullness of life to the rich and comfortable, or humility to those who are impoverished. We have nothing practical to demonstrate, which is in such direct opposition to the way in which Jesus did things that I'm amazed we've managed to keep the denial up for as long as we have.

God is interested in both faith and action. As James wrote:

What good is it, my brothers, if a man claims to have faith but has no deeds? Can such faith save him? Suppose a brother or sister is without clothes and daily food. If one of you says to him, 'Go, I wish you well; keep warm and well fed,' but does nothing about his physical needs, what good is it? In the same way, faith by itself, if it is not accompanied by action, is dead. But someone will say, 'You have faith; I have deeds.' Show me your faith without deeds, and I will show you my faith by what I do. You believe that there is one God. Good! Even the demons believe that – and shudder. You foolish man, do you want evidence that faith without deeds is useless?

James 2:14–19

We need to work hard to develop not only right belief but right behaviour as well. Of course, that's going to cost us, especially as very often it seems that God wants to bring justice into areas in which we have had injustice committed against us. I was recently thrilled to meet a guy called Bill Wilson who had been left on a street corner as a child by his mother. He stood there for three days, watching people go past, waiting in vain for his mother's return. Eventually, someone (a Christian, so it happened) took him home. They didn't give him much, but they gave him enough. He chose not to be conditioned by his conditions, but to become an agent of change in society. He now works in Brooklyn, New York, leading a Sunday school for 25,000 children who each receive a visit in their homes every week. Thousands of lives have been changed through his work. God is a comforter to those of us who need comfort, and then he invites us to go and comfort others in the way we have been comforted by him.

On a trip to Bangladesh I came face to face with two extremes. First I was amazed by the sheer size of the problem facing people: with a population of over 135 million, 85 per cent of whom live below the poverty line (eating fewer than three meals per day) there was poverty all around. Yet I was struck by the community-transforming work of the ministry that I was visiting. One of their ventures was to provide micro-enterprise loans. A work group from a community was formed, perhaps a group of wives or two or three families. They then met with a supervisor to plan their business venture and finally, when they were ready, the micro-enterprise loan was made. For the first year it was a humble 1,000 taka or $20 per individual. The loan then had to be repaid on a weekly basis; if one of the group was unwell or had a bad week of business the others in their group were responsible for meeting their repayment. My travels took me to a village called Tolna where groups were making rope out of coconut shells and beautiful patterned cloth out of thread. These micro-enterprise projects were empowering people to be creative, work together, generate income and take responsibility for each other. Now that's what I call an alternative society.

## *Life action*

1 Consider acquaintances and friends you have who live with injustice. Have you spoken to them, recognising what they live with, and asked if there is anything you can do to help?

2 Do you feel you are desensitised to injustice in the world by the way news is communicated (or not communicated) by our media? In what ways could you heighten your awareness to issues of injustice?

3 Are you a global Christian: are you a Christian who is aware of the needs of God's world and responding in countries other than your own?

Pray and pursue a friendship with a person, church or organisation involved in development work in a developing nation.

4 In what ways are the institutions and companies (e.g. bank, supermarket, school, work) that you have contact with passive or active about justice? What could you do to encourage them to be active about using their power for justice?

# 8

# *Time and Self-Management*

## The scene

Like the first cuckoo of spring, the failure of our national sporting sides and the continual presence of desperately unfunny graffiti 'artists' etching their pearls of wisdom on to the walls of public toilets, lack of time is a now familiar part of the fabric of twenty-first-century life. Some like to imagine that it's running faster, while others pin the blame on the increases in communication technology. Whatever the reason, there just doesn't seem to be enough of Old Father T around these days. Shame, that, because time, in case anyone was in any doubt, is one of the finer things in life.

So, as well as there being a sense of a lack of it, there's also too much being asked of us within what precious little we do have. From teachers to students, office workers to skilled professionals, the maturing of free market economics has meant that results are king. And if results are king, then performance and productivity are the chiefs of staff. Everyone must now jump when they say so, everything must be carried out in accordance with the mantra: make it faster and make us richer. The noble art of taking it easy, the concept of work being satisfying – worthy, even – long before profitability is considered is sadly disappearing.

Third, the pressures have spread: not only do we face them at work, but they've hitched a ride and come back home with us. Not only do we now have to achieve results during the 9-to-5, but thanks to the rise in popularity of the DIY Special, we're now supposed to live in MDF-adorned palaces where we whip up awe-inspiring meals in minutes in between landscaping the garden until it looks as if it would belong in the Ideal Home Exhibition.

A few years back there was a whole run of movies that picked over the bones of our slavery to time: *Clockwise*, *Planes, Trains and Automobiles, Groundhog Day*. Now life has imitated art to such an extent that the prospect of sitting through two hours of hectic headless-chickenery just doesn't seem like much fun. Why bother watching it on the screen when it's going on for free at home?

## A theology of time

So what on earth can the Bible have to offer on this? Is there not enough time? Genesis kicks off by telling us that in three days God created the shape of the universe, followed by three days in which he created the content, after which he rested. So right from the start we see that everything that exists has been created by God, and this includes time. God has put together both the form and the filling; he has created both time and space.

I don't believe that he was up against a deadline, that he had to pull out all the stops at the last minute to make sure things were ready on time. God is both beyond time – in the same way that he is beyond our understanding – and infinitely aware of it, able to use and work with it. It also follows that since he created both time and us, there must be an element of compatibility between the two. If God has created time and space, it stands to reason that he has created enough of it, and it also makes sense that he knows how much time we need to do the things that he asks of us.

So there is enough time. If God is perfect and he has created time, time is perfect. If time is perfect, we have got just the right amount of it.

Is there too much to do? Our lives can often seem like a plate-spinning game: then one of the plates drops and it's no game any more. The wisdom of Solomon offers us a wonderful poem about time:

There is a time for everything, and a season for every activity under heaven;
a time to be born and a time to die,
a time to plant and a time to uproot,
a time to kill and a time to heal,
a time to tear down and a time to build,
a time to weep and a time to laugh,

a time to mourn and a time to dance,
a time to scatter stones and a time to gather them,
a time to embrace and a time to refrain,
a time to search and a time to give up,
a time to keep and a time to throw away,
a time to tear and a time to mend,
a time to be silent and a time to speak,
a time to love and a time to hate,
a time for war and a time for peace.

Ecclesiastes 3:1–9

In short, there isn't too much to do. We have been promised that there is a time for everything. The challenge is, do we find ourselves doing the right things at the right time?

Is the pressure too much? Well, Jesus didn't seem to think so when he said: 'Come to me, all you who are weary and burdened, and I will give you rest. Take my yoke upon you and learn from me, for I am gentle and humble in heart, and you will find rest for your souls. For my yoke is easy and my burden is light' (Matthew 11:28–30).

The answer to the question seems to be that it depends whose yoke we are wearing. If we are carrying Jesus' yoke then the pressure won't be too much, but if it is a DIY version then the pressure might well be intolerable. If we're doing what Jesus would want us to do, we should not feel overstressed and unable to cope with it.

But, of course, we've all felt overburdened many, many times, and the trouble comes when we realise that most of the time it isn't God setting us tasks to do, but considerably less divine beings like teachers, parents and managers.

## Self-management

What we can do is to exercise control over the time that is ours. What's more, a stressful workload can be made less of a nightmare by planning, preparation and attitude. In the same way that we can control what goes into our bodies, we also have a certain degree of control over how we react and respond to external pressures.

Try drawing a table like this for yourself.

| Important and Non-Urgent | Important and Urgent | Non-Important and Urgent | Non-Important and Non-Urgent |
|---|---|---|---|
|  |  |  |  |

Done it? In each box write down the things that make demands on your time and that fit each category. For example, in your first box – Important and Non-Urgent – you might go for doing some exercise, eating healthily or sorting out your finances. Box Two – Important and Urgent – might contain things like fixing your car, hanging out with a friend who has just popped round or getting the food in for the dinner you're cooking later on. In the third box – marked Non-Important and Urgent – you might include the likes of a salesperson knocking at your door, an overflowing laundry basket or a call from someone you're not particularly keen on talking to. The final box – Non-Important and Non-Urgent – takes all the stuff like junk mail, trivial jobs round the house and so on.

Once you've filled in the boxes it's time to have a good think about things. The key to good self-management is to operate as much as possible in Box One – the things which are both Important and Non-Urgent. There will always be times when the Important and Urgent comes up and we have to operate in Box Two. However, as much as possible we should avoid living in Boxes Three and Four, which are things that are Non-Important. This way – according to Stephen Covey, the man who came up with the idea – you'll not only keep on top of your tasks, but you'll also be giving your time to the things which are Important. The ideal is not to be continually responding to and having our work dictated by interruptions. Instead, we should be determining our own priorities as much as possible. Spending time budgeting our money will help avoid the immediate screams that may come if we find ourselves in debt. Keeping fit will not only help us feel and perform better, but will also help keep many physical ailments at bay.

## Let's get practical

So how can we put this kind of theory into practice? I suppose the only way that I can suggest is by explaining how it works for me. The basis of it all is an understanding of the roles that I'm taking responsibility for in my life. I've got six of them, and I feel that some of them have been things that God has called me to while others are things I've been given and have felt it right to take. Here they are: as a person, a director, a speaker, a consultant, a coach and an author.

At some point in the year I sit down and work out what my goals are for each area. For example, as the director of Joshua Generation my aim is to build a team of people who are able to take an active role in helping a new generation rise up and fulfil their potential. That's my goal, and it's written down along with those that relate to the other five roles and responsibilities I've taken on. What I then do is use the goals as a kind of lens through which I view everything else in life. That way I'm nearly always operating in the Important rather than the Non-Urgent. That doesn't mean that I'm a slave to the goals, never able to deviate from the path. Instead, it means that I have a framework to help keep things in place.

My roles and goals are used in three ways: for making decisions, for planning, and for reviewing.

There's a big dilemma of dilemmas that faces us all:

how do we know when to say yes, and when to say no? Making decisions can be a tough one, and it's important to know where God comes in. Do we need to ask his advice on every little and large decision of the day, or have we matured in our relationship with him so that we know what he wants? Do we want God to treat us like infants or adults? The writer to the Hebrews seems to have an opinion: 'Anyone who lives on milk, being still an infant, is not acquainted with the teaching about right-eousness. But solid food is for the mature, who by constant use have trained themselves to distinguish good from evil' (Hebrews 5:13–14).

If God has given us roles in life and we have prayerfully set goals, then it makes sense that those roles and goals can be our lens through which we decide what to do and what not to do. When someone asks me to do something I consider it next to my goals, and if it fits I tend to say yes and if it doesn't I nearly always say no. Simple – well, most of the time anyway.

Having a diary is key, as having my time planned means that I'm much more likely to use it well. At the start of each week I check out what I've got on and what time I've got available. I then plan things so that at the end of each week I will have invested in each of my six roles. This is also the rule of thumb when I'm doing my planning months in advance. For example – and sticking with the Important and Non-Urgent theme – whenever I travel out of the country I always try and see my closest friends before I go away and soon after I get back.

Of course, we all get the calls on our time that are both

Important and Urgent, and it's often for them that I'll make drastic, last-minute changes. What they nearly always are, though, is relational. There's nothing more pressing than a friend or colleague in need, and at times like that the roles and goals have to move to the back burner. Some things in life are just too precious.

As well as using my roles for planning, I use them for reviewing. At the start of each month I look back over things and work out how my goals measured up with the actual results. During my summer holidays each year I sit in the sun and look over the previous twelve months' progress. I work out how things have gone in relation to my roles and goals, and it's always a great opportunity to thank God for the way I can see him working in my life.

If you're serious about managing your time you'll be serious about how you manage your R&R (rest and relaxation). I like nothing better than having an evening to open a fine bottle of wine, play some smooth sounds on my stack, light some candles and soak in a hot bath of bubbles, followed by a nice pasta and a movie. It always does the trick and leaves me clean, full and ready for bed. Sheer paradise.

God has modelled R&R for us: after six days of creating the universe he kicked back and took a day off. If we have been created in God's image then we are people who need to kick back as well.

Our bodies know when they've been working too hard, and are well practised in sending us clear signals. A friend gets headaches, while I get a dull pain in my shins whenever I'm in real need of some relaxation time. It's vital that we listen hard to these signals; if we don't, the pressure will turn to stress and the stress to burnout.

## Time opportunism

Now this kind of chapter can easily come off sounding all prescriptive, so much so that it could provoke one of two responses: 'that's for me' or 'I'm off'. But it all depends on you and your personality as to how far you want to take this stuff. If you're the more laid-back type you might want to mix and match, but if you're a tad more on the hyper side, this next bit might be for you.

I think there's something to be said for being a time opportunist, someone who makes the most of every spare moment. Time becomes the commodity as you aim to do more in less time, in order that more time might be freed up allowing you to pursue other goals and interests.

One of the keys to being a time opportunist is the double whammy: the art of pulling off two Important yet Non-Urgent things at the same time. That might mean having a business meeting while playing sport or meeting friends and eating. I'm also well into using public transport so that I can work at the same time as travelling, with the aid of one of those tiny palmtop computers. Getting one has changed my life (and I mean that sincerely, as sincerely as anyone can mean it who is hoping that someone at Psion is reading this and wants to give away a few freebies in his direction) by allowing me to be forever reading messages, sending and receiving emails or editing books like this one. Let's face it, technology is on the side of those seeking to make the most of their time.

At the end of it all, good time- and self-management is about doing things. As Robin Williams suggests in *Dead Poets Society*, seize the day. Time waits for no man, so the saying goes, but it can at least be harnessed.

### Life action

1 Do you feel you are a person who does too much or too little? Write down what you feel your roles are in life and then write goals for what you want to achieve in each of them. Use these to plan your diary for the next week, to help you focus.

2 Think back over the last week: how many Non-Important things have you done? Take some time out to pray and ponder the things that are important to you and how you can avoid the Non-Important.

3 What double whammies have you found useful in utilising time? What double whammies could you plan for the next week?

# 9

# *Church and Community*

## The scene

Let's be honest here: the face of the church is changing. That's nothing unusual, for the church has been changing ever since day one, as the people of God have been searching for ways in which to express and deepen their faith in Jesus Christ. As generations come and go, so the Church is moulded this way and that, the subtle inflections encouraged by one generation giving way to the grander reorganisations of another. But I'm thinking about something else altogether, not merely the change in style or form, in the speed of the songs or the colour of the carpet. *The Face* made clear how they felt about it all in their review of the last year of the twentieth century:

> George Orwell's famed assertion that the British aren't a churchgoing nation proved truer than ever in 1999.

141

National Sunday attendance dipped below a million for the first time since records began. For the Church of England things looked as black as a Bishop's cassock. And then came Cliff: spurned for most of the nineties, even Radio 2 wouldn't play his single 'The Millennium Prayer'. It then went to number one. This was the final and most bizarre religious manifestation of the year, but there were many more: the spiralling success of the Cannongate books of the Bible, pocket sized and with introductions by the likes of Nick Cave, Will Self and, inevitably, Bono; Christian-themed films like *Dogma*, Luc Besson's *Joan of Arc* and even Arnie's *End Of Days*; the *Guardian* reports that the Christian Union at Durham University was the fastest growing student organisation in the country; and a Christian club, Abundant, ran for a while in London's Fitzrovia. Meanwhile the government gave themselves a quasi religious makeover, incorporating a new star of Bethlehem-style logo unveiled at the party conference with the slogan 'for the many, not the few'. It was topped off by Cherie Blair's miraculous conception. Call it disorganised religion, a search for stability in the face of war, the impending apocalypse or perhaps too many drugs, people took all kinds of random pieces from belief systems they had rejected long ago. It'll all die down once we survive the New Year's eve.

They were right about the attendance figures, too; throughout the 1990s 2,200 people stopped attending Sunday church meetings each week in England. As a guide, things would have been slightly better in Scotland and slightly worse in Wales. And a thousand of those people were under the age of fifteen. This means that the Church is not only declining, but it is also greying, as more and more congregations are left with members solely from the pre-war generation.

But it's not all about numbers; the shape of the Church is changing too. Churches are beginning to adapt to consumer demand, realising that Sundays just aren't always the most convenient days for people. The rise of mid-week services has meant that the nightmare figures pointing to a mass exodus don't tell the complete story. As Alpha courses have grown, so too have the numbers attending church meetings on days other than Sundays, and the rise in the popularity of mid-week youth meetings has also done much for unofficial figures. There's a church in Cambridge that, at 4.30 on a Monday afternoon, has 250 mothers and children turning up for a service. It makes sense when you think about it, and hopefully it won't be long before we're tailoring times – if not content – to all manner of people groups.

But it's not quite the desperate scrabbling around that some might have us believe. Let's not fall into the trap of pitying the Church as we would a gently dribbling senile aunt. The Church – whom Jesus loves as a groom loves his bride – is, I believe, merely responding to the multiple changes in society. We've looked at many of those so far – time, work, family and so on – and the Church must continue to ask itself questions about the contexts in which we are church. After all, God hasn't changed, but are we so sure that our structures and systems are so perfect that they don't need to change?

## Focus

The way I see it, the Church is changing its focus. The new church movement, birthed in the 1970s and 1980s, helped us rediscover the Church as a community of people rather than as buildings. The change in focus facing us now is a shift in thinking, from perceiving church as something which happens on a Sunday in a particular place – if you like, as a gathered community – to something which takes place in the life of the members throughout the week wherever they are – as a dispersed community. Rather than meeting together to sing, pray and be taught, we will come to view church as being defined by and implemented through the acts of Christians as they go about their business out in the rest of the world. At times, the dispersed Church has very much existed to facilitate the gathered Church; now, the focus will shift as the gathered Church exists to facilitate the dispersed Church. To put it another way we have lived in the world to serve in the Church, now we will live as the Church to serve in the world.

Jesus prophesied that the temple would be flattened, that not one stone would be left standing on top of another. Later, as he was about to return to heaven, Jesus promised that his disciples would preach the gospel throughout Jerusalem, Judea, Samaria and the ends of the earth. For a while, though, the disciples stayed preaching it in Jerusalem, until 70 AD, when both of Jesus' prophecies finally kicked into gear. Not only was there a great persecution in Jerusalem, during which time the temple was plundered and flattened, but the disciples were scattered out into Judea, Samaria and then the ends of the world. I'm convinced that this persecution became a catalyst for the Church's development, meaning that instead of focusing in on themselves the members started to focus out on the world around them. The persecution was a significant trigger for the mission of the early Church as they were dispersed from Jerusalem.

So what does that mean for us? Well, I think we're living with similar themes and textures. Perhaps there is a new dispersion taking place, a reworking of the changes that catalysed the Church so radically that first time. For the last few decades we have seen the rise in numerous national initiatives to reach the United Kingdom with the gospel of Jesus Christ. Embarrassingly, the statistics have shown that we have failed miserably. Could the fragmentation of our culture be a new catalyst for the Church, driving her in mission into the world?

As the landscape of society is being transformed, the Church will be offered a choice: either go with the flow or stick to the established order of things. The thought of having church policy dictated to by cultural trends might sound odd, but there are elements of the cultural shift which we can easily embrace: placing a greater deal of importance on relationships, being prepared to re-examine truth in the light of a personal response, integrating faith with all other aspects of life. If we can get a hold of this, then the Church has the potential to have a far greater influence dispersed than it currently has gathered.

## Structure

The second change on the horizon is one of structure. For hundreds of years the Church has been working with a vertical hierarchy. Within the Anglican Church, curate has been under vicar, vicar under bishop, bishop under dean under archbishop, and other denominations have followed similar patterns. This has made for a great deal of control being kept by relatively few people. I think it's about to change, flowing with the developments that have already been seen within the business community. There we have seen a move on from similar vertical power lines to a more level playing field. Instead of a few at the top having responsibility for all, there are many more people spread out along a horizontal line of power and responsibility. Soon after Greg Dyke was installed as the Director-General of that age-old institution the BBC, he took out a level of management, so that instead of having four directors reporting to him he had twenty-four. This enabled better communication, faster decisions and greater equality. Applied to the Church, this could make for some dramatic changes. Co-operation, partnership and relationships would cross denominations and networks. There would be more horizontal relationships between churches across towns, cities and regions. Instead of churches fighting for their individual patches, there would be co-operation and partnership between churches for specific territory. There would be a greater appreciation of the diversity and variety within our faith, instead of a suspicion that others are keen to pollute our precious values with their own heresies.

## Teaching and teachers

The Church's teaching will change too. I'm convinced that if we are to grasp the opportunities open to us, we will end up having moved on from the present model of conceptual theology to something better defined as lifestyle theology. OK, so this all sounds a bit fancy, but it's really quite simple. At the moment, whenever I speak at a university I'm asked to sign the UCCF (University and Colleges Christian Fellowship) *Basis of Faith*. It's a brilliantly sound document, and in signing it I'm declaring that I'm on board with the biblical truth and the evangelical message it contains. Unfortunately, due to the nature of the document I could still quite happily sign it and be conning the Inland Revenue, sleeping with my girlfriend and shooting up on drugs every night. It may be sound, but at present *Basis of Faith* deals simply with conceptual things. I think we will soon be witnessing a shift in the Church's teaching and theology that moves beyond this type of cerebral position and on to something more practical, something more of a manifesto for life.

If the teaching is going to change, it makes sense that the teachers will change too. Mirroring the shift from modernism (which placed emphasis on absolute truth and apologetics) to a post-modern world view (embracing subjectivity, diversity and interpretation), I think we will see a shift in the way we communicate the gospel. Previously we've relied on words, particularly the exact words of the Bible. In no way am I saying that we are going to ditch it – that would be a horrendous mistake to make, and one that has been made before – but I believe that instead of spending time going through passages with a fine tooth-comb, explaining historical contexts and word derivations, we will favour other ways of teaching. We'll move from the exegetical as the primary mode of teaching to it being perhaps the secondary mode. The primary will be the use of stories, images, humour, video, vulnerability, discussion and direct application to our everyday lives.

## Relevance

The Church's relevance is bound to change, too. As we re-establish what we consider to be important, we will end up reassessing many of the things we have clung to for years. It reminds me of the adventure of Paul and Barnabas recorded in Acts 15. They're having a good old barney at a council in Jerusalem over just how right it is for the non-Jews who are becoming Christians to remain uncircumcised. Paul and Barnabas were arguing that taking such a step would be enforcing the law but missing its spirit. Faith was, according to them, enough to secure salvation, and it's a belief that we have largely kept up with to this day. Yet even though they 'won' the argument and the council agreed with them, Paul still encouraged Timothy to get circumcised so that he might not cause offence to those Jews for whom it was still a sensitive issue (how could it ever not be?). Despite being vindicated, Paul was still able to dispense with the non-essentials (or in this case Timothy's non-essential) in order to gain a hearing and communicate the gospel.

A Christian newspaper ran a feature at the start of the year 2000, asking various Christians what their hopes or prayers were for the coming century. There was a fascinating breadth of opinion, with one of the older, more established names claiming that his hope and prayer for the twenty-first century was exactly the same as it had been for the twentieth century. In one sense I agreed with him, while in another sense I found myself totally at odds with his opinion. Surely not everything about the way we ran things in the last century worked, so why on earth should we stick to the same tactics? We need to find a new relevance for the Church in our society. Interestingly, a younger guy offered the advice that we should start this century by selling up all the existing church buildings and starting all over again. He might just have a point.

## Community

The Church's community will also change as we rediscover what I think was the greatest miracle Jesus ever performed: the miracle of inclusion. He welcomed everyone to him – the lepers, women, children, poor, tax collectors, prostitutes, the exiled and the excommunicated. For all those who had been excluded and ostracised, Jesus was something completely different. Instead of playing by the old societal rules, he turned them on their heads and welcomed everybody in. I've planted a couple of churches over the last decade, and at some point in the future I'd like to do so again. I would love to start a church community for hurting, broken and disgraced people, a church that would know grace and mercy. My prayer is that the Church will practise the miracle of inclusion.

## Leadership

Church leadership will become less visible in time. This ties in with that most frequently used of metaphors, the Church as a body. Paul used it when he wrote to the Romans, the Corinthians and the Ephesians because he wanted to present a structure in which all the gifts were equal, including that of leadership. We seem to have forgotten about that and have moved on to the established hierarchies already discussed. The evangelical (biblical emphasis) and charismatic (Holy Spirit emphasis) movements are, like other sociological and cultural movements, very good at creating celebrities. A bishop I sat with one morning described it as being 'guru-ed' and suggested that it is why the Church waits until after people die before sainting them. We also see the celebrity thing within the sporting world or around a new genre in the music industry. However, as leadership becomes more invisible, the leadership of the Church in this century will be better able to facilitate, to empower the body of Christ in the world.

In North America there has been a lot of talk of the new apostolic networks, the basis of which is the ministry of the apostle as one who is sent and is a sender. You can even purchase an apostolic starter kit for a handful of dollars. These apostles are often held in high regard to the point of veneration, a bit like a saint in the Catholic Church. There is no doubt that God is upon these apostolic leaders in planting churches, as they have been one of the few groups in the USA that have seen church growth. There is, however, another angle on this new apostolic movement: it is the view that the apostolic ministry might be upon the body of Christ in order that they might be sent into the world. It is a shift from seeing the leader as hero to seeing the people of God as the hero. Paul describes it to the church at Ephesus: 'It was he who gave some to be apostles, some to be prophets, some to be evangelists and some to be pastors and teachers, to prepare God's people for works of service, so that the body of Christ may be built up' (Ephesians 4:11–12). These ministry gifts are given for the body of Christ, not for the indulgence of an individual.

## Spirituality

I think our perception of spirituality will change, too. A recent article in *The Face* magazine captured how in vogue, if unorthodox, spirituality is:

> DIY religion. Until now, there was always a clear divide between the supposed seriousness of 'proper' religion and the silliness and inconsistency of superstition. Horoscopes were sneered at as the time-wasting obsession of poor and uneducated types, while posh people looked into the future by watching the news. Traditionally, you were expected to find the religion that worked for you and stick to it. These days, straight Christianity is for old ladies, and fanaticism has made devout, singular spirituality a no-go area. Best bet, then, is to pick and mix your favourite bits: learn your fate via your Chinese horoscope, arrange your bathroom using feng shui, place your pot plants for maximum chi energy and still believe in karma, Jesus and aliens. Unlike before, no one can moan at you: a wildly inconsistent spiritual portfolio is a

sign of self-awareness and entrepreneurial endeavour. Now, the race is on to find another ancient form of massage/flower arranging/meditation that no one else in your social circle has heard of yet.

To be able to offer a distinctive Christian spirituality which is accessible and real is essential as we look to be relevant in this culture. Consequently, the way we encounter God and the way in which we develop our relationship with him is going to become less centred around a view of Jesus being some divine Superman, and more focused on his humanity. The foundation of Christianity is the miracle of the incarnation – the fact that God chose to surrender the privilege of heaven and become like one of us in Jesus Christ. The Gospel of John describes the incarnation by saying 'In the beginning was the Word, and the Word was with God, and the Word was God' (verse 1), and then that 'The Word became flesh and made his dwelling among us' (verse 14), or, as Eugene Peterson translates it, 'moved into the neighbourhood'. However, it could be said that the Church has spent the last 2,000 years trying to change what became flesh back into word again. Perhaps we have taken what God has made real and tangible in the person of Jesus and reduced him to mere words and doctrines. I'm sure that this is due for a change, and that we will rediscover some of what it means to have Jesus live alongside and with us.

One Easter weekend I did the good son thing and went on a family outing to hear Handel's *Messiah* on Good Friday at the Royal Albert Hall. It was wonderful to put my head back and listen to the beautiful words about Jesus' incarnation, crucifixion, resurrection and ascension sung. However, I was left wondering what Handel thought of the human years in between Jesus' birth and death. The following week I was speaking at Spring Harvest and part of the material looked at one of the early church creeds, again a wonderful articulation of the incarnation, crucifixion, resurrection and ascension of Jesus. Again, I was left wondering what the early Church thought about the actual life of Jesus. I believe we need to rediscover the human Jesus so we can truly ask and act on the question: what would Jesus do?

The challenge of how we meet God in everyday life is perhaps the greatest challenge for the Church of the twenty-first century. What does a new spirituality look like which will sustain, strengthen and guide people in contemporary life? Mmm . . . I think a book enabling people to encounter otherness in the ordinary things of every day might be useful . . . must chat with the publishers.

## Example

Finally, the Church's example is all set to change. In a post-Christian society, where there is no all-pervading fabric of the faith or even a vague residue to seep into the core of people's being, things will simply have to change. When people have no experience of Christianity, when it's as alien and unfamiliar as Morris dancing, then the only Bible that people will be reading and the only Jesus they will see is in the way we live our lives. The only basis on which they will judge the faith is the very people who claim to follow it. That means you and me. Oh dear.

But perhaps this isn't a cause for alarm after all. Perhaps this is the fresh start that some have been looking for. At least if people are unsure about an institution they may be a blank canvas when it comes to forming an opinion about how a friendship with God impacts their lives. As my articulate friend Chris puts it,

> The Church exists so that God can demonstrate what he wants the world to be like so that the gospel can be observed operating in a genuine society which, in its loving unity of spirit, in its diversity of culture, personality and thought, in its glorious creativity exemplifies the image of God and what it means for creation to be set free from futility.

The calling on the Church is the same as the calling that Israel had: for a chosen community to model life in God to the communities that surround it. The challenge is to live in such a way that others want to follow the same God. The nation of Israel failed; how is the Church of the twenty-first century going to do?

When I'm speaking to groups I sometimes get people to play a kind of 'Simon Says' game. I bunch my fingers up, getting people to do the same, and ask them to place their hand on their chin. Despite the fact that I ask people to aim for the chin, I'll place my own hand on my cheek. You know what happens? Virtually everyone places their hand on their cheek. You see, people are far more inclined to do what you do rather than what you say. Good news for the Church in the twenty-first century? You decide.

### Life action

1  As a part of a church, how could you contribute to helping people live in your community to serve in the world, rather than live in the world to serve in the Church? Perhaps you could initiate the discussion in your community.

2  Make some time to reflect upon your life as a Christian and then write down what other people might imagine.

3  Ponder the ways that you encounter God day by day. Are there ways that you could do more of the things in which you find you encounter God? Where in your life do you struggle to encounter God? Imagine what it would be like and what it would take for you to meet God in those aspects of your life.

# Conclusion

If being a disciple is to be a learner, then Pete was one of the most notable. He was often so far away from having got it together that he has become the champion for many of us lost causes and repeat offenders. He was the rock who was as solid as jelly, and on the day they first met Jesus knew it straight away. He turned to him and announced that he 'will be called Cephas' (John 1:42), which means 'rock'. Jesus knew how frail, human and fickle he was, and I think his tongue was firmly in his cheek when he delivered the line.

We see him as the guest who refused to be served (John 13:6–9) when he refuses Jesus' offer of a quick foot-spa. In John 13:21–6 we find out about his taste for gossip, trying to wangle out of John who Jesus meant when he talked about being betrayed by one of the twelve. A few verses on and we're able to see him as the follower whose words are just a little more ambitious than his deeds. He claims he'd die for his master, but Jesus points out that he'll actually deny him three times within a matter of hours. Nice one, Pete.

In the Garden of Gethsemane, when Judas turns up to lead the soldiers to arrest Jesus, our man Pete is there to save the day. He draws his sword and with a mighty blow . . . strikes off some servant's ear. It makes you wonder where he got his sword from; after all, in the three years he had been hanging out with Jesus there hadn't been an awful lot of armed conflict – not, at least, that we're told about. His aim was well sketchy and didn't even cut down one of the soldiers: he managed to damage the hearing of the High Priest's servant. OK.

Then there's Peter the friend, who does a nice line in denial. Read John 18:17, 25, 26–7, and there you see the three occasions on which he claimed not to know Jesus. He was also pretty poor when it came to running as, three days after the crucifixion, he and the other disciples hear that the tomb lies empty. He and 'the disciple whom Jesus loved' (I wonder which Gospel that appears in?) decide to run there, and guess who comes last?

He was a poor fisherman, as John 21 makes clear. He was at it all night with no success, which for a fisherman was probably just ever so slightly embarrassing. The next day up comes Jesus – the trained carpenter – and offers a little advice. It turns out that Pete is only yards away from success, and on taking the stranger's advice (and a carpenter's at that) and casting his nets on the other side, he hits the jackpot.

Does Pete make you feel like a disciple? It works for me. He reminds me of me when I blow it by saying and doing the wrong thing. There are three things that stick out from his life. First up, let's be honest: we don't know it all and we haven't got all the answers. Anyone who thinks they have is going to be surprised. Second, we're all going to make mistakes, and we'll only learn from some of them. Sometimes we'll make the same mistake three times. Finally, it's good to know that discipleship is all about entering into a bigger adventure than we've ever known before. It's full of love, fun, laughter, amazement and vulnerability. I'm sure that Jesus still laughs at his disciples, just like he did with Pete.

**Matt Bird** and the **Joshua Generation** team work with churches and organisations in the UK and around the world to help them invest in the new generations and to reinvent themselves in new cultures.

Joshua Generation
The Church Worple Road
Wimbledon
London
SW19 4JZ

Tel: 020 8947 1313
Fax: 020 8947 9414
Email: admin@joshgen.org
Web: www.joshgen.org

Also by Matt Bird with Craig Borlase

# Destiny

### *Discover the Life you were Created to Live*

At one of the most critical points in the history of humankind, God selected Joshua to succeed Moses and lead the Israelites into the Promised Land. An ordinary man, called to an extraordinary destiny.

This is a book about discovering your own destiny, and developing the character you will need to fulfil it. Matt Bird believes that God has a life-changing purpose for every one of us, and that we must prepare ourselves to take on the mantle of the previous generation. In DESTINY, he describes the seven essential values of tomorrow's history-makers.

*'Matt's radical message will inspire you to fulfil your calling for the twenty-first century.'*
MIKE PILAVACHI

*'The need to encourage and envision young adults has never been greater . . . I wholeheartedly endorse the work of Matt Bird.'*
SANDY MILLAR

Hodder & Stoughton
ISBN 0 340 75616 0

Mike Pilavachi with Craig Borlase

# For the Audience of One
## *The Soul Survivor Guide to Worship*

Worship is great: the music, the dance . . . but isn't there
more to it than that? Does God enjoy it as much as we do?
What happens when the music stops?

Worship is not something we do for our own benefit. It is for
God, the audience of one. We should be worshipping every
minute of every day, and we don't need words or even a tune.

Soul Survivor is at the heart of the incredible revival in
contemporary youth worship. FOR THE AUDIENCE OF ONE
shows that, beneath the surface level of words and music, a
phenomenal work of God – anointed, culturally relevant and
biblically sound – is taking place, enabling people to be broken,
healed and transformed by him.

This book should be read by everyone with a desire to
go deeper in their worship, and includes a special section
for worship leaders.

Mike Pilavachi is the founder of Soul Survivor and
pastor of Soul Survivor, Watford, UK.
Craig Borlase is a freelance writer.

Hodder & Stoughton
ISBN 0 340 72190 1

Mike Pilavachi with Craig Borlase

# Soul Survivor Life

The aim of the SOUL SURVIVOR LIFE series is to explain the
basics of Christianity and Christian living in down-to-earth,
jargon-free language. The four books follow the pattern of
life: birth, adolescence, mid-life crisis and death.

The first, WALKING WITH A STRANGER, explores what it really
means to become a Christian, who God is and how we can
build a personal relationship with him. MY FIRST TROUSERS looks
at the challenges and rewards facing us when we start going
deeper with Jesus. The Christian life is not easy, however, and
WEEPING BEFORE AN EMPTY TOMB asks how to cope when the
going gets tough. The final book, AFTERLIFE, is about facing the
future, in particular death, heaven and eternity.

All published by Hodder & Stoughton

WALKING WITH A STRANGER: ISBN 0 340 73534 1
MY FIRST TROUSERS: ISBN 0 340 73535 X
WEEPING BEFORE AN EMPTY TOMB: ISBN 0 340 73536 8
AFTERLIFE: ISBN 0 340 73537 6

David Westlake

## Soul Survivor Presents

# Upwardly Mobile
*How to Life a Life of Significance*

There's more than one way of getting yourself
upwardly mobile.

The glossy mags will give you all the advice you need for a
fast-track route to flash cars, crisp suits and a seat on the board.
But God's blueprint for life has rather different goals: feeding
the hungry, sheltering the poor and loosening
the chains of injustice.

It's not quite as difficult as it first sounds. You don't need money,
power or fame to become a person of significance in God's eyes.
UPWARDLY MOBILE will help you discover your potential to
make a real difference in the world in which we live.

UPWARDLY MOBILE is the first book by David Westlake,
youth director of Tearfund.

Hodder & Stoughton
ISBN 0 340 75654 3